SPARKY'S RETURN

Andersen Young Readers' Library

DAVID WEBB

SPARKY'S RETURN

Illustrated by Karen Elliott

Andersen Press · London

Text © 1987 by David Webb
Illustrations © 1987 by Andersen Press Limited

First published in 1987 by
Andersen Press Limited,
62-65 Chandos Place, London WC2

British Library Cataloguing in Publication Data
Webb, David
   Sparky's return—(Andersen young
readers' library)
   I. Title   II. Elliott, Karen
823'.914[J]   PZ7

ISBN 0-86264-165-9

Printed and bound in Great Britain
by Anchor Brendon Limited, Tiptree, Essex

Contents

1
The New Arrival

'Now I want you all to make Simon feel welcome,' said Mr Boyling as he stood before the fourth year junior class of St. Gregory's C.E. Primary School. 'Help him to settle in quickly—show him how friendly we can be here at Thornley.'

The new arrival, looking most uncomfortable as he faced a sea of staring unfamiliar faces, smiled weakly at the Head Teacher and muttered: 'Thank you, sir.'

'You'll like it here,' said Mr Boyling. 'We've got a good set of children—with one or two notable exceptions. I'm going to leave you with Mr Watson now. He will sit you next to someone who will look after you.'

'Don't worry, Mr Boyling, we'll sort him out,' said Wacky Watson, putting a reassuring hand on the boy's shoulder. He waited until the Head Teacher had left the room and then turning to face the class he announced: 'This is the new boy I told you about. His name is Simon Parks and he has just come from the South to live in Thornley.'

The figure that stood in front of the class was a strange one. Simon Parks was small for his age and was pathetically thin. He had a shock of red hair and numerous freckles to match, some of which were magnified by a pair of brown-rimmed spectacles with thick lenses. His clothes didn't help his appearance, for as if to complement his hair he wore a bright red jumper and maroon trousers which didn't seem to fit him properly. Stuart later told him that he looked like a stringy carrot with glasses on. Many of the children were too stunned by his appearance to laugh, but there were one or two sniggers emerging from behind exercise books.

The new arrival just stood there, pushing his glasses further up his nose every so often, waiting for Mr Watson to make the next move.

'Right,' said Wacky Watson using one of his favourite words. 'You can sit next to Stuart, he'll keep his eye on you.'

'Aren't you the lucky one,' whispered Michael Jones, who sat directly behind Stuart. 'You'll need sunglasses if you're going to keep your eye on him!'

The new arrival was shown to a block of six wooden desks grouped together near the back of the class. Stuart pulled his chair out for him and he sat down looking totally embarrassed.

'Don't worry,' said Stuart quietly, 'you'll soon settle in here—I'll show you round at break.'

'Thanks, that would be nice,' muttered the new boy, and he pushed his glasses up and folded his arms.

The bell for morning break sounded at ten thirty, and the children jostled with each other to get out of the classroom as quickly as possible. It was a fine spring morning, warm for early April, and they were keen to get out into the bright sunshine.

'Come on, then,' said Stuart. 'Let's have a look at the place. What did you say your name was?'

'My name's Simon—Simon Parks,' said the new boy following Stuart into the corridor. 'You can call me Sparky if you like—that's what they used to call me at my last school.'

'All right,' said Stuart trying to keep himself from smiling, 'if that's what you want. Where have you . . . .'

'Come from?' said Sparky, finishing the sentence for him. 'Oh, I've moved around. My father is researching at the army base up on the moors outside Thornley. I don't even know how long I'll be staying here. I've been in more schools than I can remember.'

'I bet you've never been in one like this,' said Michael joining them near the top of the stairs. 'The teachers here say it's got character; if you ask me it should have been pulled down years ago.'

'Take no notice of him,' said Stuart. 'It's our centenary year, you know. The school is a hundred years old in June. In fact, we're . . . .'

'Mounting a big display in the hall,' said Sparky, looking up at the paint flaking from the ceiling.

'How did you know that?' asked Michael. 'I suppose old Boiler has been spouting again.'

'No, I've not really spoken to Mr Boyling,' said Sparky making his way down the steep stone stairs. 'The yard is through the hall, isn't it?'

'We've got a strange one here,' whispered Michael as

9

the two boys followed the vivid red shape down the stairs and out through the hall.

Once they were in the playground Sparky became quite a centre of attention. Many of the younger children buzzed around him like flies, but Sparky didn't seem to bother. Indeed, he seemed to take everything in his stride, and he spent the entire playtime wandering around the school yard looking up at various parts of the building. Stuart and Michael followed in his footsteps, chasing off the younger ones every so often. At one point Sparky stopped in front of the great stone wall that bordered the playground and turning to Stuart he demanded: 'Where have the toilets gone?'

'What do you mean where have they gone?' replied Stuart, looking puzzled. 'They haven't gone anywhere as far as I know. They're at the end of the corridor at the bottom of the stairs.'

'Unless someone's run off with them,' said Michael seriously. 'Someone might have run off with them, you know.'

'I think you're wrong,' said Sparky pushing his glasses up his nose, and off he went again across the playground.

He hadn't gone more than a few paces when he was stopped by a large, ugly-looking boy with a mass of untidy black hair. The boy, who was chewing gum, stood right in front of Sparky, blocking his way, and as Sparky tried to walk around him the boy took a step sideways so that there was no way past.

'What's your name, Carrot?'

'My name's Simon Parks, but most people call me Sparky.'

'Sparky!' said the boy, almost spitting the word out. 'Sparky! What sort of a name is Sparky?'

'It's my name,' said Sparky, looking at the boy as if he was stupid.

'You're not trying to be . . . .'

'Funny?' said Sparky, finishing the sentence.

'Are you taking the . . . .'

'Micky out of you?' said Sparky, as the boy grabbed his jumper. 'No, I don't mean to mock you—it just happens.'

'Leave him alone, Spike,' said Stuart stepping in between them. 'He means no harm, it's just his way.'

'Well, I don't like it, see?' said Spike, blowing a large, pink bubble from his mouth. 'He'd better watch himself.'

Wacky Watson was on playground duty and as he approached Spike made off in the opposite direction, glaring back at Stuart and Sparky as he blew another huge bubble.

'You want to keep well away from him,' said Stuart. 'That's Tommy Milligan, but we call him Spike and if you've got any sense you'll keep out of his way.'

'Not very pleasant, is he?' observed Sparky. 'I was only looking around.'

The whistle blew for the end of playtime and as the children filed in Spike removed the sticky pink gum

11

from his mouth and flicked it at Sparky.

Tommy Milligan was always getting into trouble at school. He was one of those boys who thought that rules were for everyone but him. The gum was an example of this, for it had been banned from school months ago when Mr Boyling had found a piece stuck on his door. Everyone knew that Spike had done it, but nobody was brave enough to tell Mr Boyling. Some of the things Spike did were amusing, but he could be really nasty at times. One of his favourite tricks was tripping up the younger children as they ran past him—the harder they fell the more Spike laughed.

Back in the classroom Wacky Watson settled the children down to work and then said: 'Have you settled in all right, Simon? Are you managing to . . . .'

'Find my way around?' completed Sparky. 'Yes thanks, sir. As a matter of fact I feel quite at home.'

'Oh . . . yes, well . . . right,' said Mr Watson, and he walked away a little at a loss for words.

Stuart and Michael grinned at each other. Secretly, Stuart thought that this new arrival might turn out to be quite a bit of fun.

It was dinner-time when Sparky had his next encounter with Spike. The children had collected their dinners from the hatch and had taken them to their places. Sparky wasn't really sure where to sit so he followed Stuart and Michael and when they sat down he joined them.

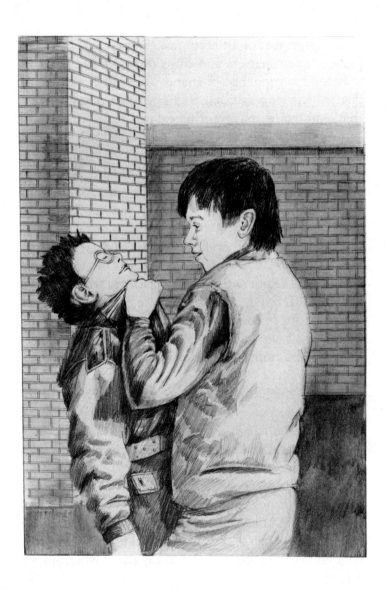

'Is it all right if I sit here?' asked Sparky, putting his plate of spam fritters and chips down on the table.

Before anyone had a chance to answer Spike appeared, chewing as usual, and said: 'Get out, Carrot—that's my place you're sitting in!'

'I'm sorry,' said Sparky beginning to rise. 'I wasn't sure where to sit.'

'It's all right, Simon,' said Mr Boyling, suddenly appearing on the scene. 'You stay where you are. I'm sure Thomas won't mind finding another place for today.'

'But sir,' protested Spike, 'I always sit there—it's my place, sir!'

'Well you're not sitting there today, are you, lad?' said the Head Teacher raising his voice. 'And what's that you're eating? You shouldn't have anything in your mouth until we have said our Grace.'

Spike said nothing for a moment and then began: 'It's only a . . . .'

'Piece of bubble gum,' finished Sparky without thinking.

Stuart and Michael stared at him in horror. Nobody at St. Gregory's dared to get Spike into trouble and they couldn't believe that Sparky had spoken up against him. Michael leaned across to him and whispered: 'You've really done it now, you have!'

'Remove it!' ordered Mr Boyling, glaring at Tommy Milligan. 'Ask one of the dinner ladies to find you a table on your own and then come to my room when you've finished your lunch.'

With that the Head Teacher stalked out of the hall, a look of anger on his face.

Spike turned to face Sparky. He was furious—his face was almost as red as Sparky's jumper.

'I'll see you later,' he said, and he removed his bubble gum slowly and deliberately from his mouth and flicked it onto Sparky's dinner before walking away.

The three boys at the dinner table just stared at the pink blob that had settled on Sparky's spam fritter.

'It looks like something from space,' observed Michael, and then he added: 'You wouldn't have liked our spam frisbees anyway.'

'He'll look like something from space by the time Spike and his gang have finished with him,' said Stuart. 'What did you have to go and say that for, Sparky? I told you to have nothing to do with Spike.'

'I can't help it,' said Sparky adjusting his glasses. 'It's just a habit I've got—I can't stop myself.'

'Spike's got a bad habit,' said Michael. 'He flattens people and turns them into spam fritters.'

'Look,' said Stuart seriously. 'You'd better walk home with me tonight, because if Spike's annoyed . . . .'

'He's going to come looking for me,' finished Sparky.

'You're doing it again!' said Michael getting excited. 'Why don't you let people finish what they're saying? Just shut up and listen!'

'Sorry,' said Sparky, and he turned over his spam fritter with his knife.

15

The rest of the day was uneventful. Spike had been kept in over dinner-time and again during afternoon break, and so he had not had a chance to find Sparky. They sat nowhere near each other in class, and although there had been a few threatening looks Spike was unable to exact his revenge during lesson time.

In addition to being a thoroughly nasty character, Spike was none too bright, and when the bell sounded for the end of the afternoon session he had done so little work that Wacky Watson made him stay behind to finish off. Stuart was relieved that they wouldn't have to meet Spike outside and he hurried Sparky away from the classroom. Sparky himself seemed totally unconcerned, and as they passed through the school gates he pushed his glasses up his nose and said:'What's all the hurry? I was going to have another look around the building.'

'You don't seem to understand,' said Stuart grabbing hold of his arm, 'if Spike gets hold of you he'll . . . .'

'Make mincemeat out of me,' said Sparky as he set off down the road.

'That's right,' said Stuart, running to catch him up. 'Mincemeat if you're lucky! And if you think Spike's unpleasant you should see the other two he hangs around with after school—they're really charming.'

'Well, thanks for your advice,' said Sparky, adjusting the position of his glasses once again. 'You've been a big help today.'

'Listen, where do you live?' asked Stuart. 'Perhaps I can call for you in the morning—save you coming to school on your own?'

Sparky stopped for a moment, scratched his head and then said:

'No . . . no, I don't think that would be a good idea. I'll tell you what—I'll call for you, shall I?'

'You can if you want,' said Stuart looking puzzled. 'I just thought . . . .'

'Yes, you were trying to help,' said Sparky. 'Weaver Street, isn't it? Number twenty-one, I think?'

'That's right,' said Stuart. 'But how did you know?'

'I've got a good memory,' replied Sparky with a grin. 'I never forget a number or a face. I have trouble with names sometimes, but I usually get them in the end.'

The two boys had arrived outside the corner shop on Royal Street. Although it was really a newsagent's it was one of those shops that sold everything—sweets, toys, groceries—you could even take shoes for repair at Thompson's newsagent's. Sparky stopped near the window and stared at the array of goods on display. He put his hands in his pockets and looking over his glasses he said, more to himself than to Stuart: 'You know, it hasn't really changed that much.'

Stuart looked in the window and then at Sparky and said: 'What hasn't changed?'

'I'll see you in the morning then,' replied Sparky, and off he went down Royal Street, adjusting his glasses as he walked, leaving Stuart staring after him wondering just what to make of this strange new arrival.

17

Stuart was not the most punctual of boys—especially first thing in the morning. He had forgotten to tell his mother that someone might be calling for him on the way to school, and when there was a knock on the front door at half past eight the following morning it did not enter his head that it might be Sparky. Stuart's mum opened the door and stared at the small, red boy standing in front of her. Sparky stared back for a minute, and then pushing his glasses further up his nose he said:

'Good morning—I wonder could you tell me if Stuart is ready to come to school yet?'

'He's just finishing his breakfast,' said Stuart's mum. 'You'd better stand inside for a moment.'

'Yes, I suppose I had,' said Sparky, and he stepped into the hall, looking all around him as he did so.

'If you just wait there, he'll be out in a minute,' said Stuart's mum, and she disappeared into the kitchen where Stuart was busy scraping the last of his cornflakes from his bowl.

'Stuart,' she said, sounding a little puzzled, 'there's the most strange boy waiting for you in the hall—speaks with a strange accent and looks red all over.'

'Oh yes,' said Stuart jumping up. 'That will be Sparky. He only arrived yesterday, but Spike's after him so I said he could call for me.'

'Well, I don't know why you want to make friends with him, he doesn't look your type at all.'

'I have to admit—he's different,' said Stuart, and he grabbed his jacket and school bag and went out to

18

meet Sparky.

'How did you enjoy your first day at St. Gregory's?' asked Stuart as the two boys walked to school.

'First day?' repeated Sparky. 'Yes, of course. I enjoyed it very much apart from Spike, but I think things could get far more interesting yet—far more interesting.'

Stuart looked at his new friend. He did say some strange things, but maybe he was right—maybe things were going to get more interesting now that there was a new arrival at St. Gregory's.

2

More About Sparky

For weeks the *Thornley Chronicle* had been reporting a spate of burglaries in the town which were proving somewhat of an embarrassment to the local police. It was obvious that the break-ins were not the work of professional thieves for the goods stolen were the sort of items that would attract young people, and on several occasions the houses burgled had been badly vandalised with furniture smashed and paint sprayed on the walls. The police knew that youngsters were to blame but despite all their efforts they had not been able to catch the culprits. Extensive press coverage had led to demands from the public for results, and the police had responded by visiting all the local schools in the hope that someone would give them a lead. It was with this intention that P.C. George Short had approached the Head Teacher of St. Gregory's, and Mr Boyling having readily agreed, P.C. Short now stood before the twenty-six children that made up Wacky Watson's fourth year junior class.

'I want you to realise that the situation is serious,' said P.C. Short, who despite his name was a huge, stocky figure well in excess of six feet tall. 'Your home could be the next one these clowns get into. It could be your bedroom that is wrecked by these louts, and it could be your valuables that are taken.'

Wacky Watson stood in the background with his arms folded, nodding in agreement every so often.

'You have got to realise,' continued the policeman, 'that it is in your interest to help us. Now, let me ask you a question—what do you think you could do to help?'

There was silence for a minute as the children searched their brains for an answer. Michael looked across at Stuart and shrugged his shoulders. Jenny Peters, who sat on the same table scratched her head and yawned. Wacky Watson fidgeted uncomfortably, hoping that his class was not going to let him down. Eventually Sparky put his hand up, and seeing a red arm waving in the air P.C. Short said: 'Yes, lad—speak up.'

'We could all write to our M.P. and ask him to press Parliament for an increased police force,' said Sparky. 'It's a well-known fact that the service is stretched to its limit and can't cope with an ever-increasing crime rate.'

P.C. Short put his thumbs behind the lapels of his jacket and stared at the boy in amazement.

'That's a very good answer, lad, but I was thinking of something . . . .'

'A little more practical,' said Sparky adjusting his glasses. 'Yes, I was quite aware of that.'

'We could all keep a lookout for anyone behaving suspiciously,' said Emma Parker, a small prim girl who usually came up with a sensible answer. Wacky Watson's face broke into a broad grin and he nodded his head up and down vigorously.

'That's just the answer I'm looking for,' said the big

policeman. 'If you all keep your wits about you we'll have this lot caught before they can cause any more damage or distress.'

'We could make sure we always keep our doors and windows firmly locked,' continued Emma, beginning to enjoy herself, 'and if we know that our neighbours are away on holiday or out visiting we could keep a special watch on their houses.'

Wacky Watson, now beaming with pleasure, nodded his head up and down again.

'I hope you all heard that,' said P.C. Short. 'This young lady has made some very sensible suggestions.'

'Load of rubbish!' muttered Spike from the back of the class, and Wacky Watson was on his feet immediately.

'Thomas Milligan—if you've got anything constructive to say by all means say it, otherwise keep quiet!'

'It's all right, Mr Watson,' said the huge policeman as he slowly made his way to the back of the class. 'I'm used to comments like that from ignorant children who think they know it all.'

Towering over the slumped figure of Spike, P.C. Short bent down and glared straight into the boy's face.

'I'll remember you,' he said, as Spike glared defiantly back. 'I'm sure we're going to meet again some day.'

The policeman thought that this action was bound to have a shocking effect on the rest of the children, but much to his consternation, as he made his way back to the front of the class he was followed by an outbreak of giggles, for there, stuck onto the policeman's bottom was a huge blob of pink bubble gum.

When Wacky Watson realised what had happened he was horror-struck.

'Silence!' he shouted angrily. 'Be quiet, all of you!' And turning to the bewildered policeman he said quietly: 'Do you think I could have a word with you outside as a matter of urgency?'

'Of course,' replied P.C. Short, and turning to face the class he wagged his finger and said: 'The message is clear—if you see anything or if you hear anything, you let me know. That's all I'll say for now, but I'll be paying you another visit in the not too distant future.'

And as the policeman triumphantly left the class, twenty-six pairs of eyes were focused on the seat of his pants.

Later that same afternoon saw the start of a strange series of events. Wacky Watson had split the class into groups to research some aspect of the school's history and in this particular lesson all the groups were concentrating on the Second World War years. Sparky had been put to work with Stuart, Michael and Jenny, and the four children were searching through a pile of old newspaper cuttings trying to find out what effect the war had on the people who lived and worked in Thornley. As they worked their way through the yellowing papers it became evident that Sparky was something of an expert at history. One particular edition of the *Thornley Chronicle*, dated 5th September 1940, contained a whole series of pictures showing how the children of Thornley coped with the war, and Sparky pored over the pages, his glasses slipping off his nose on several occasions.

'Look at that little girl,' said Jenny pointing to a small, square picture that had caught her attention. 'What's she got on her face?'

'That's her gas-mask,' replied Sparky. 'Didn't you know—everyone had to carry a gas-mask and they used to practise taking them on and off at school. It was in case the Germans dropped poison gas. The children had to carry them around in a special box.'

Michael prodded Jenny with his pencil and said: 'You'd look better in a gas-mask.'

'Look at this picture of an Anderson shelter,' said Stuart turning the page. 'I bet it was great spending the night in one of those. Imagine lying there listening to the enemy planes flying over.'

'Of course it wasn't great,' said Sparky, almost snapping the words out. 'It was freezing cold and it was wet. Insects crawled over you as you sat there shivering—you couldn't sleep because of the noise from the enemy planes. How can you say it was great?'

'All right,' said Stuart, rather taken aback. 'Keep your hair on. I just thought it sounded exciting, that's all.'

Sparky had turned another page and was staring at the headline to one of the major news items of that week. At the top of the page in bold, black type were the words:

'AMMUNITION TRAIN HIT—HUGE EXPLOSION.'

'I've heard about that before,' said Michael. 'My grandad's told me about that incident. He was an air raid warden at the time and he says he was at Thornley Station when the train blew up further along the line.'

'That's very interesting,' said Wacky Watson suddenly appearing behind the group. 'Why didn't you tell us about your grandfather before, Michael? Maybe he could come in to talk to us—there's nothing like a first-hand account of events and I had planned to invite some speakers into school.'

'Oh, he'd talk all right, sir. The trouble is you can never shut him up once he starts! He goes on for hours. The ammunition train being bombed was one of the first stories I can remember him telling me. I must have only been about three and I used to sit on his knee while he droned on about the war—my mum said it was a sure way to get me asleep. Anyway, the Germans bombed this train just as it was coming over Thornley railway bridge. My grandad said the explosion was . . . .'

'Deafening,' chipped in Sparky suddenly. He was still staring at the page, and even though his glasses had slipped off the end of his nose he made no attempt to adjust them. 'It was deafening,' he continued. 'And there was more than one explosion—there were a whole series of explosions as trucks went up—and the shrapnel—pieces blown all over Thornley—you could feel the heat, and people were screaming, they didn't know what had happened.'

'You've got a good imagination, Simon,' interrupted Mr Watson. But Sparky took no notice of him and carried on speaking in stuttering, broken sentences, still staring down at the old newspaper as if in a trance.

'He's gone all sweaty,' said Jenny as she noticed the perspiration gathering on Sparky's forehead.

'They couldn't get near the survivors—it was the bridge, you see—partly blown away—and there were people screaming through the smoke and chaos . . . .'

Sparky's voice was getting louder and higher in pitch, and at this point Wacky Watson grabbed hold of his arm and said: 'Are you all right, Simon? Are you feeling unwell?'

'What?' said Sparky, shaking his head and sitting back in his chair. 'No, no—I'm fine, really. I just had this strange sensation—I went all cold.'

'Cold,' repeated Jenny, pushing her long hair from her eyes, 'you looked all hot and sweaty.'

'Anyway, I'm all right now,' said Sparky. 'It was probably something I ate—forget it.'

Stuart looked hard into Sparky's eyes as Wacky Watson wandered off to talk to one of the other groups, but nothing else was said and the incident was soon forgotten as the children settled down to continue their research.

It was Tuesday, the day the school computer club met in the library after lessons had finished. Michael and Jenny were not in the least bit interested in computers, but Stuart attended every week without fail and he was more than pleased when he found out that Sparky shared his interest. The club lasted for about an hour and this particular session the older fourth year children were showing some of the younger ones how to write simple games programmes. As with all his lessons, Sparky seemed to have natural ability and he handled the computer with ease.

Every so often Spike would appear outside the library. Wacky Watson chased him off several times but before too long he would return to grimace through the window and press his face against the glass. To make matters worse he was joined by some dirty-looking older boys, one wearing a tatty brown leather jacket and the other a particularly ugly boy who had a permanent grin and was covered with spots. Spike's friends led him on, laughing and shouting and generally encouraging him to make a fool of himself.

'They're the ones he hangs around with,' said Stuart as he and Sparky pulled their coats on ready to go home.

'They look a bright bunch,' observed Sparky, as the three of them chased each other round outside the library, tripping each other up and rolling over and over on the ground.

'I think we could do with slipping out of school while they're occupied,' said Stuart. 'I've got a nasty feeling Spike might just be waiting to introduce you to his friends and I'm not so sure you'd like to meet them.

Come on—we can leave by the side entrance.'

The two boys grabbed their bags and made their way along the corridor to the school's side entrance. Stuart stuck his head out first and seeing that the way was clear he turned to Sparky and said: 'Let's get a move on then, before they realise what's happened.'

Everything seemed to be going fine, but just as the two boys reached the school gate Spike appeared from around the side of the building, his friends close behind him.

'They're getting away!' shouted Spike. 'Let's get after them!'

'Run for it!' yelled Stuart, and he grabbed hold of Sparky's arm and hauled him out of the gate.

The two boys ran for all they were worth up the back alley leading to Royal Street, Spike and his unsavoury gang chasing after them screaming and yelling like a demented dog pack.

Just as the boys reached the corner shop Sparky stumbled, catching his foot on an uneven paving stone, and he went sprawling to the ground, landing in a crumpled heap by the wall, his glasses flying off and into the nearby gutter. Stuart stopped as soon as he realised what had happened, but he could see immediately that he was too late to help Sparky, for Spike's gang were almost upon him. As they came out of the alley the youths stopped running and walked slowly towards Sparky who was groping around on the ground in search of his glasses. Spike spat out his bubble gum, pointed to

Sparky and said to the ugliest of his gang: 'Get him, Moggy! Show that carrot who rules round here!'

Moggy stepped forward, clenched fists protruding from his leather jacket, and was about to deliver his first blow when a stern voice boomed out: 'I shouldn't do that if I were you, lad!'

Stuart turned in his tracks to see the reassuring bulk of P.C. Short appear from the doorway of the corner shop.

Moggy turned away immediately to join his friends, who were already backing away down the alley.

P.C. Short didn't utter another word—he just stood there looking threatening.

'We'll see you two again,' said Moggy, pointing first at Stuart and then down at Sparky. Then the gang turned and sauntered off down the alley shouting back comments as they went.

P.C. Short bent his huge frame and helped Sparky up from the pavement, as Stuart recovered his glasses from the gutter.

'Are you all right?' asked the big policeman.

'Yes thanks,' replied Sparky. 'My glasses are a bit scratched, though.'

'You're lucky it's nothing more serious than a pair of scratched specs,' said P.C. Short. 'They're a nasty lot— you'd do well to keep away from them. Anyway, off you go home, lads. Your parents will be wondering where you've got to.'

Sparky dusted himself down, pushed his glasses

firmly onto his nose and set off at a brisk pace down Royal Street, Stuart following close behind him.

'You've had quite a day again,' said Stuart, catching up as they were about to cross into Weaver Street. 'In fact, you've caused quite a stir since you arrived at St. Gregory's. I don't know . . . .'

'What's going to happen next,' completed Sparky, stopping abruptly. 'No, I don't suppose you do, but we'll see in the morning, won't we? I'll call for you as usual, shall I?'

And without waiting for a reply Sparky set off down the road once more, waving his arm in the air by way of departure.

3

Spike Takes His Revenge

The following morning Stuart overslept a little and Sparky was once again knocking on his front door before he had finished his breakfast.

'Will you get a move on?' shouted Stuart's mum. 'That strange boy is here already—you're going to be late for school.'

'You mean Sparky,' replied Stuart, shoving a piece of toast and marmalade into his mouth. 'Let him in for a minute, will you?'

Stuart's mum opened the front door to be greeted by a shock of red hair sticking out of a maroon anorak.

'Is he late again this morning?' asked Sparky. 'I'll come in for a minute, shall I?' And without waiting for a reply he stepped into the house and started looking around. Stuart's mum shook her head and led him into the kitchen.

'Morning, Sparky,' said Stuart gulping down his last mouthful of tea. 'I'll be with you in a minute—just got to do my teeth.'

Stuart left the room and then stuck his head back round the door and said:

'I was telling Mum how much you knew about the ammunition train. She said her uncle was the driver—he was killed in the explosion.'

'Mr Bannister?' said Sparky, looking surprised. 'You

knew Mr Bannister?'

'No, I never knew Uncle Joe,' replied Stuart's mum. 'He was killed well before I was born, but I've heard the story of the ammunition train many times. Anyway, how come you . . . .'

'Know so much about it?' finished Sparky. 'I just have a good memory for facts, that's all.'

'Let's go, then,' said Stuart grabbing his bag as he passed through the kitchen. 'We're just going to make it in time.'

It was five minutes to nine and as school started promptly at nine o'clock the two boys had to run. They dashed past the shop on the corner of Royal Street where Sparky had so nearly come to grief the previous evening, and as they sprinted up the back alley which came out opposite the school Sparky shouted somewhat breathlessly: 'There's something wrong, Stuart.'

'What do you mean?' asked Stuart, slowing down and waiting for Sparky to draw level with him.

'You'll see—at school I mean.'

As the boys came out of the alley a police car drew up near the school gates and two policemen got out.

'I told you,' said Sparky, 'there's something wrong.'

The two policemen made their way through a crowd of chattering parents who had gathered just outside the school gates, and the boys followed them into the playground. Groups of children were standing around pointing up at the building, and as Stuart raised his eyes to follow their gaze he let out a gasp, for virtually every

33

window in the upper storey was smashed.

'There's been a break-in,' said Jenny coming over to join them. 'It's supposed to be a right mess inside. We've all got to go straight to the school hall when the bell goes.'

The bell was ten minutes late that morning, presumably to allow the caretaker and staff to finish clearing up the broken glass that littered classrooms and corridors. When the children entered the building they were shocked at the extent of the damage. Despite the caretaker's efforts there was paper everywhere—most of it display work that had been ripped from the walls, and the walls themselves were streaked with red and black spray paint. Lights had been smashed and doors had been kicked in, including the door to the library where the computer equipment was stored. As Stuart and Sparky walked past on their way to the hall they could see that the floor was littered with books, many of them torn to shreds or bent and crumpled beyond recognition. It was as if a madman had entered the library and gone berserk, wrecking everything he could get his hands on.

The children were not kept long in the hall. Mr Boyling informed them that much of their equipment was badly damaged and that several items, such as cassette players and the portable television had been stolen, along with a supply of felt tip pens and a small amount of petty cash. The police were investigating the incident and as far as he was concerned school would carry on as normal. It would take more than a group of mindless vandals to put St. Gregory's out of action.

When the children went back to their rooms it became apparent that the classes had not been too badly affected, although sprayed in large black letters across the back of Mr Watson's room were the words 'WACKY IS A DIMWIT'. Books had been torn from the shelves and thrown across the room, and of course, there was no glass in any of the windows. Wacky warned the class to look out for splinters of glass and then the children were set to work reading while Mr Watson and one or two of the girls tidied up as best they could. After a few minutes, Jenny leaned across her desk towards Michael and said quietly: 'I can't help but notice that Spike's not in this morning.'

'Well, you're not sorry about that, are you?' replied Michael. 'We're better off without him.'

'What she's trying to say,' explained Sparky peering over his reading book, 'is that Spike's absence is particularly suspicious in view of this morning's events.'

'You don't really think Spike is responsible for this lot, do you?' asked Michael sounding surprised.

'Spike would stoop to anything,' said Stuart joining in the conversation. 'He tried to introduce Sparky to some of his friends on the way home last night. It was only thanks to P.C. Short that we got away without a good thumping.'

'Shouldn't we tell someone, then?' asked Michael. 'You heard what P.C. Short said—keep our eyes and ears open for anything suspicious.'

'But we haven't seen or heard anything,' said Sparky, rubbing his glasses with a grubby-looking handkerchief. 'We're just guessing at the moment, and until we have some definite information I suggest we say nothing.'

And as if to end the conversation, Sparky placed his glasses firmly on his nose and buried his head in his reading book.

That evening after school some of the boys had agreed to meet for a game of football up at the Parish Mill Fields. Sport was one of the few things Sparky hadn't got a clue about and he found football a particularly pointless game.

'It's a waste of valuable energy,' he complained to Stuart and Michael as they made their way out of Thornley and up towards the playing fields. 'If you're lucky you end up hot and sweaty and covered in mud, if you're unlucky you limp home with cuts and bruises.'

'What are you coming up for then?' said Michael. 'You don't have to come, you know.'

'I'm coming because I've got nothing better to do,' replied Sparky. 'Anyway, I'm not going to play. I'll watch from the side.'

'Well if you want you can . . . .'

'Be the referee?' finished Sparky. 'I think I'll go for a walk around the fields and meet you afterwards, if you don't mind.'

When they reached the Parish Mill Fields the game had already started. Stuart and Michael left their coats with Sparky at the side of the pitch and wasted no time in joining in. Sparky watched them for a while, a gaunt red shape standing on the sideline with his hands thrust deep into his trouser pockets, but he soon got bored and his attention began to wander. Even with his glasses Sparky's eyesight left much to be desired and as he looked around he was attracted by what appeared to be a large stone building at the top end of the neighbouring field, which sloped steeply away from the football pitch. Sparky's curiosity was aroused, and forgetting all about the coats left in his charge, he ambled off to investigate. As he neared the building his eyes began to focus more clearly, and he could make out that it was some sort of large shelter or view point, hexagonal in shape with wooden bench seats inside.

'Ah, yes,' he muttered as he slumped down onto the hard wooden seat, 'it's all coming back to me now.'

The shelter provided quite a vantage point. From where he sat Sparky could see the blurred figures of his friends playing football and beyond was Thornley itself, its disused mill chimneys outlined against the sky like silent monuments to the past. At one time Thornley had been a productive mill town at the heart of the South Lancashire cotton industry, and the vast majority of its working men, as well as many of its women and children were employed in the mills and factories. The raw produce was shipped into Liverpool, the great west-facing port, and then on to Thornley via the ship canal. The town had once throbbed with the noise from the factories, and every morning the workers had poured from row upon row of tiny houses and clattered down the cobbled streets towards their place of work. But the decline of the industry had led to the decline of Thornley, and as Sparky looked down on the empty mills, it was like looking at a vast museum preserving monuments to a bygone age.

Suddenly the silence was broken. Sparky was aware of voices and he knew instantly that one of the voices belonged to Spike, and he realised that he was separated from the voices only by the thin wall of the shelter. Sparky pushed his glasses firmly onto his nose, sat absolutely still, and listened.

'They haven't got a chance,' said Moggy. 'I'm telling you, they haven't got a chance!'

'When are we splitting them?' asked Spike. 'I could do with some of the felts.'

'We don't split anything yet,' replied Moggy. 'I'm telling you, they all stay in the store till I say.'

'But there's loads of stuff in the store,' said a voice Sparky didn't recognise. 'It's time we got rid of some of it—make room for the next lot.'

'They stay in the store till I say. If you don't like it you can . . . .'

'Find someone else to work with,' blurted out Sparky, and he bit his tongue and braced himself for the reaction.

'Did you say something?' asked Moggy, looking threateningly at Spike.

38

'It wasn't me, Moggy,' said Spike. 'I think it came from the other side of the shelter.'

'Check it!' snapped Moggy, and before Sparky could even get to his feet he was faced by Spike and the large spotty youth who bared his teeth and grinned like a skull.

'It's Carrot!' said Spike in surprise. 'He's been listening, Moggy!'

Moggy sauntered up to Sparky, hands in pockets, and looked him straight in the face.

'That wasn't a good idea, was it, Carrot? Me and my friends don't like people spying on us—especially little red creeps like you.'

'I just came up here for a walk,' stammered Sparky. 'I didn't know you were here. I've been watching the football game.'

Moggy took a step forward and prodded Sparky with his forefinger.

'Well you'd better go back down, hadn't you?'

At this point Moggy slowly and deliberately removed Sparky's glasses, dropped them on the floor and ground them into the dirt with his boot. Sparky stared down helplessly at the broken bits of glass and brown plastic.

'I'm telling you, you didn't hear or see nothing—right? One word from you and you'll end up like your specs, so keep your . . . .'

'Mouth shut! Yes, I'll make sure I do that, Mr Moggy. Thank you very much.'

Sparky rose gingerly and backed out of the shelter. He

seemed unsteady on his feet now that he no longer had the use of his glasses.

'He can prove nothing,' said Moggy confidently as they watched Sparky stumble down the field towards his friends. 'Even if he talks he can prove nothing—he didn't hear enough.'

The football game had just finished and Stuart and Michael were surprised to see their coats left unattended.

'Now where's he gone?' said Stuart looking round the field. 'He seems to come from nowhere and disappear into thin air when you need him.'

'Here he comes,' said Michael, pointing towards a blurred red shape stumbling down from the shelter. 'He looks like a giant tomato rolling down the hill.'

'What on earth is the matter with him? Why is he walking like that?'

Stuart sounded concerned and as Sparky blundered closer and closer towards them the reason for his stumbling became clear.

'Sparky,' said Stuart, 'you've lost your specs. I suppose they've fallen off your nose somewhere and you can't see well enough to find them.'

'Well, yes . . . and no!' said Sparky, pausing to get his breath back. 'I mean, I have lost my glasses but they didn't exactly fall off.'

Michael scratched his head and looked at Stuart.

'Sparky, I don't suppose you'd like to . . . .'

'Explain what I mean? Yes, of course I would. I went up to the shelter, you see—did you know, by the way, they used to use that shelter as a lookout post in the war? There used to be an air raid siren, and what's more . . . .'

'Get on with it, Sparky,' snapped Stuart impatiently.

'Yes,' said Sparky, and he raised his hand instinctively to adjust his glasses which were no longer there. 'I was just sitting in the shelter admiring the view when I heard Spike and Moggy and that spotty youth who keeps grinning. They were discussing some stolen goods they've got stored away. I think Spike is getting a little impatient—he was going on about sharing out packs of felt tips—probably taken from our school. Anyway, Moggy told him that they were to stay in the store, and I didn't mean to say anything but it just came out!'

'I see,' said Michael, 'and they smashed your specs, I suppose?'

'Well Moggy took them off—I couldn't really see what happened next, but I know for sure now that they are the ones responsible for all the recent break-ins. They've obviously got a secret store somewhere where they hide the goods they steal.'

'Right,' said Michael, 'so we go and tell the police.'

'Wrong,' replied Sparky, raising one finger in the air. 'I know for sure that they are responsible but there is still no real proof. It's my word against theirs, and that is just not good enough.'

'But we can't get any better proof,' said Stuart. 'Not unless we catch them red-handed with the stolen goods.'

'Exactly!' said Sparky, and his face broke into a broad grin.

'You don't mean you heard them say where their store is?' asked Michael.

'Oh, no . . . I didn't hear anything like that,' replied Sparky. 'They were just discussing how they were going to share out the goods.'

'Well if we don't know where their store is how can we catch them red-handed?'

'But I do know where their store is,' said Sparky. 'I know exactly where their store is. I suggest we do nothing for a few days—let Moggy forget all about me. We'll leave it until Saturday and then go along to the store and take a look.'

'Perhaps you'd like to tell us where this store is?' said Stuart, not at all sure that Sparky knew what he was talking about.

'If we can get hold of some of the stolen items we'll have all the proof we'll need,' said Sparky, completely ignoring Stuart. And without saying another word Sparky set off across the football pitch back down towards Thornley, almost falling over a clump of grass as he went.

'What did you make of that?' asked Stuart as he and Michael stared after the stumbling red shape.

'I think he's a nutcase,' said Michael firmly. 'I'll tell you now—there's no way I'm going into Moggy's store if it exists. No way whatsoever!'

43

4

Bailey's Ghost

'All right,' said Michael, trying to sound disinterested, 'I'll come along with you, but there's no way I'm going into the store. Anyway, Sparky, you haven't even told us where it is yet. I'm beginning to think you're making it all up.'

'Of course I'm not making it up,' said Sparky indignantly. 'I've told you—I know where they've got the stolen goods stored, and if you come along with me tomorrow morning I'll show you.'

'I'm coming along too, you know,' said Jenny as the four children walked across the playground at the end of an eventful week at St. Gregory's.

'But you're a girl,' said Michael scornfully.

'It's very nice of you to notice,' replied Jenny, flicking her long hair from her eyes, 'but it doesn't alter the fact that I'm still coming with you.'

'Let her come,' said Stuart. 'She can stand watch outside the place while we go in and investigate.'

'You don't listen to a word I say,' protested Michael. 'I am not going into the store—if we ever find it, that is. I can't see the point of walking into the lion's den, or the Moggy's den in this case!'

'Well, if you're too scared,' replied Jenny, 'you can stay on watch while I go in with Sparky and Stuart.'

'Who said anything about being scared?' protested

44

Michael. 'This is ridiculous—we don't even know where this place is and we're arguing as to who should stand watch!'

'Anyway, where are we going to . . . .'

'Meet tomorrow morning?' finished Sparky, adjusting his new glasses, which fitted him every bit as badly as his old ones. 'I suggest we get together outside the corner shop on Royal Street. It's only about ten minutes' walk from there. Is nine thirty all right for everyone?'

'I think I can manage that,' said Stuart.

'Me too,' added Jenny.

'I suppose so,' grumbled Michael. 'But it all sounds like a waste of time to me.'

'That's fine,' said Sparky, grinning with satisfaction. 'Nine thirty it is then!'

Michael was late. In fact, the other children were about to go without him when he came dashing down Royal Street with half a jam sandwich in his hand.

'This really is ridiculous,' he panted, coming to a stop outside the corner shop. 'I could be doing something useful like sleeping or watching television.'

'Let's see what we can find,' said Sparky, completely ignoring Michael's comments. 'We're going up to Oak Street—shall I lead the way?'

'Oak Street?' said Jenny in surprise. 'I didn't think there was anything left of Oak Street. I thought all that area had been pulled down and cleared ready for the new shopping precinct.'

'A lot of the property has gone but part of Oak Street is still standing. Let's go and take a look, shall we?'

Sparky set off at his usual brisk pace leaving Stuart, Michael and Jenny to follow in their own time. His hands were dug deep into his anorak pockets, and as he led the way through the strets of Thornley he seemed oblivious to everyone and everything. Every so often he whistled to himself—the old war songs 'It's a long way to Tipperary', and 'Pack up your troubles in your old kit bag'—and he occasionally turned round to check that his friends were still following him.

'He's a nutcase,' said Michael as they struggled to keep up with Sparky, 'a real nutcase!'

As Sparky continued his journey through the streets of Thornley the surrounding property began to get more and more dilapidated until eventually they were passing derelict houses and pieces of wasteground where the buildings had disappeared altogether.

'It looks like a scene from the Blitz,' said Stuart looking round at the piles of masonry and heaps of rubble. 'It's just like some of those war pictures we've been looking at.'

'For goodness' sake, don't say that to Sparky,' snapped Michael, 'you'll start him off on one of his fits again!'

Amidst the ruins stood Oak Street, partly demolished but in remarkably good condition compared to the rest of the area, and at the far end of Oak Street stood a huge, concrete building that had once been the Classic Cinema. The sign from the front of the building had all but disappeared, a few odd letters remaining hanging loosely across the entrance. The entrance itself was boarded up as were the windows, and the boards were covered with graffiti and old bill posters advertising events long past. It was to this building that Sparky led his companions, and stopping outside the main entrance he turned to face them, adjusted his glasses and announced: 'Here we are then—the Ritz Cinema.'

'The Ritz!' stammered Michael. 'This isn't the Ritz, it's the old Classic. Don't tell me we've come all this way for nothing! He's brought us to the wrong place!'

'No, no, no . . .' said Sparky getting agitated, 'I assure you this is the right place. The stolen property is hidden inside the Ritz.'

'Listen,' said Michael, walking up to Sparky and poking him in the chest with his forefinger, 'this cinema is the Classic—or at least it was! It's been closed and boarded up for years and I know a very nasty tale about this place. Nobody in their right mind would set foot in there—not even you! The place is haunted!'

Jenny looked at Stuart and Stuart looked at Sparky, and two demolition workers in donkey jackets walked past and looked at all of them.

'What do you mean "haunted"?' asked Sparky after considering his words carefully.

'I mean,' said Michael, lowering his voice, 'that inside the cinema there is a ghost—a very nasty, malevolent ghost at that, and there is no way I'm going inside to get frightened to death.'

47

'I don't think I believe in ghosts,' said Jenny with a gulp, 'but if there is a ghost, how did it get in there?'

'Well,' began Michael, 'rumour has it that a madman called Bailey escaped from the psychiatric hospital up on the moors. He had an obsession for horror films and he came along to the Classic every night for two weeks until he was recognised by the manager. Of course, the police were sent for and when they raided the cinema Bailey fled to the projection room and locked himself in. When the police tried to force the door open he murdered the projectionist and then committed suicide himself. It was soon after that the cinema closed. People kept feeling uncomfortable in the place. It's said his ghost still haunts the building, waiting to break out of the projection room and take revenge on anyone who dares to encroach on his territory.'

There was silence for a minute as the children stood in the spring sunlight and considered the tale, and then Sparky said: 'I have never heard anything so ridiculous in my life! Let's go round the back. I think we will find we can enter the building through one of the fire exits.'

'I'm afraid I agree with Sparky,' said Jenny, not in the least impressed by Michael's story. 'If you believe that rubbish you'll believe anything.'

'Well I didn't say I believed it, did I?' said Michael, somewhat taken aback. 'I'm just repeating what other people say.'

Michael set off after Sparky and the others, determined now to enter the building to prove that he wasn't really afraid.

Sparky had no difficulty in finding the fire exit. Around the back of the building was a flight of six stone steps and at the bottom of the steps was a pair of doors that had once been green but now had very little paint left on them. They were the type of doors that were operated by a push bar from the inside, but even before they descended the steps the children could see that there was a gap between the doors where one of them had been forced open.

'Come along, then,' said Sparky, 'let's take a look.'

Stuart put his hand on Sparky's shoulder and holding back for a moment he said: 'Sparky—how did you know we'd be able to get in through this fire exit? In fact, you haven't explained . . . .'

'How I knew about the cinema? No, I haven't, have I, but there's time for that later. I suggest we satisfy ourselves that the stolen goods really are stored here, and then we can go and explain everything to the police.'

'If you don't mind, I think I will wait outside for you,' said Jenny, suddenly feeling rather nervous now that the time had come to enter the building.

'That's fine,' said Michael. 'I'll remember you to Bailey's ghost.'

The boys made their way down the broken stone steps, kicking away the tin cans and litter that had been tossed there. Stuart put his foot against the first of the doors and there was a scraping, jarring noise as it slowly jerked open. Inside it was pitch dark and even before they entered the boys were aware of a dank, musty smell. Michael peered into the darkness and said: 'I don't think I'm so keen on this after all.'

'We've come this far,' said Stuart, 'we may as well follow it through.' And he stepped inside, beckoning Michael and Sparky to follow him.

The boys stood just inside the doorway for a minute, waiting for their eyes to adjust to the darkness.

'We should have brought a torch,' said Sparky. 'This is as bad as the blackout when the sirens sounded.'

'What on earth are you talking about?' asked Michael, keeping his voice down to a whisper.

'Never mind,' said Sparky, 'let's make our way further in.'

The boys were able to make out that they were in a narrow corridor, and a short distance in front of them was what was left of another door. It appeared to have been kicked in, for the bottom section was dented and splintered and it hung loosely from its hinges. Beyond the door was the great rectangular room which had formed the main viewing area and as the boys entered, it was like stepping into a vast, empty relic of the past.

They found themselves in the bottom left-hand corner of the cinema, The floor sloped upwards away from the screen and at first the boys moved slowly and cautiously, but as their eyes grew accustomed to the darkness so their co-ordination improved and they were able to progress into the building without fear of stumbling.

The place had an eerie atmosphere about it. Every sound seemed to echo around the huge empty room which was bitterly cold, the only hint of the spring sunshine being the occasional shafts of light that penetrated the blackness from cracks in the damaged roof or upper walls.

The boys stopped for a moment to get their bearings. Behind them was what remained of the huge screen, once pure white, now stained and marked and daubed with graffiti. One torn curtain hung limply across from a decaying beam. The floor was quite rotten and they had to tread carefully for fear of it giving way. As they advanced slowly towards the back of the cinema they were faced by row upon row of folding seats, many with their backs and cushions slashed almost beyond recognition. About halfway up the aisle Michael stopped and whispered: 'I think we're too early for the film—there's no one here yet!'

'What are you whispering for?' whispered Stuart.

'It just seems the right thing to do in this place,' replied Michael, his voice still low.

Sparky sat down on one of the few seats that was still intact and gazed down towards the screen.

'The old Ritz.' he muttered, more to himself than to his friends. 'Who would have thought it would end up like this.'

'I'm sure you've got it wrong,' said Michael, a little more confidently now that he had got used to the building. 'You're in the old Classic—there's no such place as the Ritz in Thornley.'

'The number of people who must have spent happy times in this building,' said Sparky, taking no notice whatsoever of Michael. 'They were fabulous some of the old films—all time greats. People must have come from all over the town to spend an evening here. There wasn't much to smile about in the war but at least the old Ritz let them escape from their trouble for a couple of hours.'

'Do you know,' said Stuart, sitting himself down in the seat next to Sparky, 'you come out with the most weird things sometimes. Just where do you get all your information from?'

Sparky seemed to shudder and come to his senses again and he said: 'I don't know that I can tell you. I seem to be able to store information—visual information—I see pictures in my mind—it's as if they're happening here and now. I can almost see and feel the people from long ago sitting here.'

'I told you,' said Michael impatiently, 'he's a nutcase. Let's get on with it.'

'Wait,' said Stuart, suddenly grabbing Michael's arm. 'What was that?'

'I didn't hear anything,' replied Michael, whispering again. 'For goodness' sake, let's get going.'

'No, Stuart's right,' said Sparky, standing up and moving back into the aisle. 'I thought I heard a noise.'

'What sort of a noise?' asked Michael, his voice

betraying a hint of nervousness.

'Listen,' whispered Stuart. 'It's there again. It's coming from behind us, from the back of the cinema.'

The boys remained absolutely still, frozen like statues in the darkness, and as they listened a faint scraping, shuffling sound could just be heard from somewhere near the back of the cold, empty hall.

'I think,' whispered Sparky, slowly and deliberately, 'that the sound is coming from the area where the projection room is situated.'

Michael could feel the skin tightening at the back of his neck, and although he was shivering he was aware that a sweat had broken out on his forehead. His mouth was dry and with great effort he whispered hoarsely: 'Did you say . . . the projection room?'

Sparky didn't answer, he just nodded his head, his eyes remaining fixed towards the back of the cinema. And then there was another noise, louder and clearer and dreadful as it echoed around the deserted cinema. From the back of the aisle, beyond where the children stood, came a creaking, grating noise that seemed to expand and grow in the darkness. Stuart and Sparky couldn't move. Michael was absolutely petrified, for he could just make out the rectangular shape of the projection room door as it slowly grated its way open. Then suddenly a dazzling bright light shot down the aisle and the children instinctively raised their hands to shield their eyes. The action seemed to jerk them into life and Michael let out a yell and screamed: 'It's Bailey's ghost—

let's get out of here!'

The echo was taken up in the emptiness and as the children tore back down the aisle towards the fire exit Michael's words rained down on them. Stuart was the first to reach the area in front of the screen and he turned momentarily to check that he was not alone. As he did so Michael charged past him and the beam of light from the back of the cinema outlined Sparky just as he let out an almighty yell and went tumbling over the remains of a broken seat. Stuart was about to go to his aid when he felt Michael's hand grip his jacket and pull him into the short corridor leading to the exit.

The last thing Stuart remembered as he burst into the daylight was the sight of Sparky sprawled on the decaying wooden boards before the screen, his hands shielding his eyes from the relentless light that was bearing down towards him.

5

Aladdin's Cave

Outside the cinema Jenny was beginning to get bored. She had been walking up and down whistling to herself, soaking in the warm spring sunshine, glad that she had decided not to explore the building with the boys. She had walked the length of the building three or four times and was just approaching the fire exit when Michael and Stuart burst through and onto the stone steps.

'What on earth's the matter?' asked Jenny, rushing to the top of the steps. 'Where's Sparky? Has he had an accident?'

'It's Bailey's ghost,' gasped Michael, the sweat pouring from his brow. 'He's got Sparky—he's going to take his revenge on him.'

'There was a light,' explained Stuart, joining Jenny at the top of the steps, 'a great beam coming down towards us from the back of the cinema. I hate to admit it, but it did seem to be coming from the projection room.'

'I'm telling you, it was Bailey's ghost,' shouted Michael, and he flapped his arms up and down in frustration. 'You wouldn't believe me, would you? He's picked out his victim in a beam of light and I hate to think what horrible fate Sparky has met.'

'Just hold on a minute,' said Jenny, remaining quite calm and completely unaffected by Michael's performance. 'As far as I can remember I've never heard of a ghost using a light. For all we know Sparky might be . . . .'

'Perfectly all right!' said a familiar voice from the bottom of the steps. 'Of course I'm perfectly all right!'

Michael stared down in disbelief at the untidy red figure below him. Stuart just grinned with sheer relief and said: 'So Bailey's ghost hasn't got you after all?'

'Er . . . no, he appears to have missed me this time,' said Sparky grinning back at his friends.

'But the light,' said Michael, 'it was coming straight towards you.'

By way of answer Sparky raised his right hand and with an outstretched forefinger beckoned his friends to follow him. Michael responded immediately, walking mechanically down the steps as if he were hypnotised. Jenny glanced at Stuart who shrugged his shoulders and they followed Michael, eager to know the solution to the mystery light.

The children made their way along the short corridor and passed through the broken door into the main hall of the cinema, and there, not more than a couple of metres in front of them stood the most curious looking old tramp who was still clinging hold of the powerful spotlamp he had used to pick out Sparky.

The tramp was dressed in a long, black overcoat which was tied loosely around the waist with what appeared to be a pyjama cord. From beneath the coat baggy trousers sagged down onto a pair of odd shoes, one brown, one black. On his head he wore an old woollen hat which at one time must have been bright yellow but was now faded and stained and seemed to complement his grey beard and straggly hair perfectly.

'May I introduce you to Bailey's ghost,' said Sparky, gesturing towards the tramp.

'Beggin' your pardon,' said the tramp in an accent that contained a hint of Irish, 'but the name's Benji, not Bailey. And might I be asking you what you're doing in my cinema?'

'Oh, this is your cinema, is it?' said Stuart looking round. 'Well I must say, I don't think much of the decoration.'

'Well, it isn't exactly mine,' explained Benji, 'but I live here anyhow, and I like to know who it is prowling about my property, see?'

'Do you know you nearly frightened us to death,' complained Michael, his voice quite steady again. 'We thought the place was haunted for a minute.'

'Haunted, is it?' said Benji, scratching his head. 'Well I don't know about that now, but I do get some very strange visitors at times.'

'Surely you don't stay up in the projection room,' said Michael, horrified at the thought of anyone living with a ghost. 'Don't you know what happened in there?'

'I know lots of things as happened there,' said Benji, 'but none of them bothers me over much. Anyhow, you come along with me and I'll give you a guided tour of my quarters. Come on then.'

58

Benji shuffled off up the aisle towards the back of the cinema and the children followed him, not quite know- ing what to expect. As they neared the projection room Michael glanced up at the small square opening from which the films were projected, and somehow his own story seemed less realistic now that the ghost had failed to make an appearance. Benji turned right at the top of the aisle and proceeded to make his way down some steps which were covered with the remains of a red carpet. The steps led to the foyer where popcorn, sweets and cigarettes had once been for sale, and there behind the counter was an old, dirty-looking mattress covered with part of the screen curtain which acted as a blanket.

'This is my bedroom,' said Benji proudly. 'Pretty good, eh?'

'Very nice,' said Jenny, trying to hide her distaste. 'It looks a very nice bedroom indeed.'

Benji was delighted that the children seemed so impressed and spurred on by his success he proceeded to take them through to a small back room behind the foyer which had probably been used as a store.

'This is me kitchen,' explained Benji. 'I've got me own cooker, as you can see.'

The cooker was a small primus stove balanced on a wooden box in the corner of the room. On top of the stove was one small saucepan, misshapen through age and grimy through lack of care and cleaning. On the floor nearby stood an equally misshapen tin kettle and it was obvious that these two inadequate pieces of kitchen equipment were the only cooking utensils the old tramp possessed.

Nearby were two more wooden boxes, one covered with an edition of the *Thornley Chronicle*. Stuart guessed that these served as table and chair as he could see a battered looking tin plate, complete with knife and fork, on top of the *Thornley Chronicle*. There was also a bowl which contained the remains of a stiff, grey looking substance that was probably meant to be porridge, and a filthy-looking mug complete with cold tea dregs. The teabag had been carefully lifted out and placed to one side ready for use the next time Benji required a drink. Several empty milk bottles completed the scene and as they hadn't been rinsed they filled the small room with a rancid, sickly smell.

'It's all very impressive, Mr Benji,' said Sparky pushing his glasses further up his nose and trying to cover his mouth at the same time. 'Tell me, how long have you lived here in the old Ritz?'

'The old Ritz!' said Benji, sounding surprised. 'Why I haven't heard it called that since just after the war. In fact, it was 1947, yes—I'm sure it was 1947 when they changed the name to the Classic. I reckon they thought "Ritz" sounded too much like "Blitz"—gave people bad memories, I reckon. Now what made you refer to it as the Ritz? You look far too young to remember that name.'

Sparky looked uncomfortable. He fiddled with his glasses again and his face looked even redder than usual.

After a moment's hesitation he said: 'I think I must have got it from one of the old newspapers we have been studying back at school. We're doing a project about Thornley, you see, and we've been looking back to the war years. I'm sure I read something about the old Ritz.'

Stuart nodded, quite satisfied with Sparky's explanation and as if to back him up he added: 'It's all very interesting. We've been reading about the night the ammunition train blew up. It turns out one of my relations was killed in the explosion.'

'The ammunition train,' repeated Benji, pulling at his beard as he remembered the terrible night. 'That's a night that will live with me for the rest of my life. They used to let me sleep in the old station waiting room sometimes—I was there the night the train went up.'

'The whole place shook,' said Sparky. 'It was like an earthquake.'

'The whole town shook that night,' said Benji. 'Anyway, that doesn't tell me why you're snooping round my quarters! Surely that's not connected to your project?'

'Not exactly,' explained Stuart. 'Sparky thinks there are some stolen goods hidden somewhere in the cinema. There have been a series of break-ins all over Thornley recently—even our school was broken into. Sparky thinks your quarters are being used as a store for stolen property.'

Benji was looking very uneasy and his fingers twitched all the time Stuart was talking. He turned his back on the children and muttered: 'I haven't stolen anything—least not this year. I don't know what you're on about.'

'We didn't say you had stolen anything, but you see—I know that there are stolen goods hidden in this cinema. I know, Benji.'

Benji paused for a moment and then he turned round and looked straight at Sparky.

'It's them louts,' he said, his voice trembling as he thought about them. 'They threatened me—said they'd wreck my quarters and have me thrown out if I opened my mouth. I don't want any trouble, see? I don't bother other people and I've no wish to be bothered myself, but they threatened me!'

'Are you going to show us where the stuff is,' said Stuart firmly, 'or shall we go and find it for ourselves?'

'I suppose you may as well know,' sighed Benji. 'It's in the projection room.'

'You won't get into trouble, Benji,' said Stuart. 'We'll make sure you don't get into trouble.'

'Let's go and have a look, then,' said Michael, completely fearless now that he knew Bailey's ghost was only a harmless old tramp.

The children retraced their steps through the foyer until they reached the solid door of the projection room. It was slightly stiff but with a bit of effort Stuart and Michael managed to pull it open, and as the light from the foyer flooded into the cold, dark room what a sight met their eyes! It was like looking into Aladdin's cave, for there were all sorts of treasures adorning the small

room, many of the items crammed into cardboard boxes. The range of goods was enormous, from clocks and watches to kettles and toasters, from framed pictures to pot plants, from a box of felt tips to one of the school's cassette players. There was enough evidence in that small room to get Spike and his friends put away for a long time.

'What a hoard,' said Michael. 'They must have been collecting this lot for months.'

'They have been,' said Benji, appearing at the door behind the children, 'but they've been getting greedy lately. They're going to . . . .'

'Get their fingers burned!' completed Sparky. 'Yes, I'm afraid they are, Mr Benji. I think P.C. Short might be very interested to see this little collection.'

'Did I hear you mention an officer of the law?' asked Benji, twitching his fingers nervously.

'I'm afraid so,' said Stuart. 'The police are going to need to take over here, there's nothing else we can do, but we'll make sure they know how much you've helped us.'

'I think I'll go and do a bit of tidying up,' said Benji, and he disappeared smartly before anyone could say another word.

'What do we do now?' asked Jenny. 'Can we go back outside, it's freezing in here?'

'I think the next step is a trip to the police station,' said Stuart, pushing closed the heavy projection room door. 'I suggest we go straight away before Spike and his friends turn up—I've had enough of this place myself.'

The children made their way back through the cinema hall and out through the fire exit into the welcoming spring sunshine. Stuart, Michael and Jenny chatted exitedly on the return journey through the back streets of Thornley, but Sparky strode on ahead, just as purposefully as he had done earlier that morning.

The police station was not that far away from St. Gregory's School and when the four children poured through the door into the small reception area they were met with a very hard stare from a severe looking policeman standing behind a large counter. The policeman was scribbling something down onto a plain notepad and didn't look too pleased at the sudden interruption.

'What can I do for you, then?' he asked, putting his pen in the top pocket of his jacket.

Sparky stepped forward, adjusted his glasses and said: 'We'd like to speak to P.C. Short, please. We have some vital information for him.'

The stern policeman leaned forward and looked at each of the children in turn, his eyes finally fixing on Sparky.

'P.C. Short is off duty today. If you've got anything to say you'd better say it to me.'

Sparky glanced round at the others and then decided to continue.

'It's about the Thornley robberies,' he said, 'we know where the stolen goods are being kept; they're being stored in the old Ritz cinema—I mean the Classic—they're in the projection room.'

'What's more,' interrupted Michael, 'we know who has been responsible for the robberies, including the break-in at our school.'

'Just hold on a minute,' said the policeman, removing the pencil from his pocket again. 'Before you start making accusations I think we'd better take some details. You can start by giving me your names and addresses.'

The children provided the policeman with all the information he required, including the name of their school, but when he asked how they had come to discover where the stolen property was hidden Sparky became most agitated and said: 'If you don't mind me saying so, officer, I feel we are wasting a great deal of time. I'm sure these minor details can be sorted out after the goods have been recovered.'

The policeman looked furious, and slamming his pencil down on the counter he glared at Sparky and said: 'I hope you're not trying to tell me how to do my job, son, because if I find you've been snooping around derelict buildings I might have a lot more questions to ask yet.'

'Sparky meant no harm,' said Stuart. 'It's just that Moggy and his gang—they're the ones responsible for the robberies—could go back to the cinema at any time. We're only trying to help you catch them red-handed.'

'Well, you wait here a minute,' said the policeman,

replacing the now broken pencil in his top pocket once more. 'I think I'd like to take a look at this projection room for myself. You'd better come and show me.'

The policeman disappeared into a back room and within a minute he emerged with a young policewoman who smiled at the children kindly. Jenny couldn't help wishing that she was accompanying them back to the cinema instead of the surly officer who now ushered them out of the station towards a waiting car.

'My name's Brock, by the way,' said the policeman as he held the car door open for the children, 'and I warn you now, I . . . .'

'Don't like having your time wasted,' finished Sparky as he settled into the police car. 'No, I'm sure you don't, and the sooner we get to the Ritz the sooner we can all get home for some dinner.'

P.C. Brock slammed shut the car door, his face almost as red as Sparky's hair. He climbed into the front, snapped on his seat belt and started the car. Not a word was spoken as they made the short journey through the town and the children felt most uncomfortable as the vehicle pulled up in what was left of Oak Street, the huge shell of the Classic Cinema looming up in front of them.

'Well?' enquired P.C. Brock as the children stood on the pavement before the front entrance.

'It's round the back,' said Sparky and off he went at his usual pace towards the fire exit at the back of the cinema. P.C. Brock followed, the other children trailing behind. When they had all gathered by the top of the steps at the fire exit Sparky said: 'It's inside,' and he led the way down the stone steps into the deserted cinema.

As they entered the main hall P.C. Brock looked around at the ruin and decay. In front of the huge yellowing screen he could feel the rotten floorboards creaking under his considerable weight and he moved quickly into the aisle.

'I hope this is worth while,' he muttered as he spotted the projection room and headed straight towards the heavy door.

The children followed, quietly confident that the surly policeman would soon change his tune and they stood back in satisfaction as he pulled open the door and stared inside. P.C. Brock turned to face them looking angrier than ever.

'You have got some explaining to do!' he stormed. 'What is the meaning of this wild goose chase?'

The children looked totally bewildered. Sparky stepped forward to show the policeman the array of stolen property and as he looked into the projection room his mouth dropped open in amazement, for apart from an old cardboard box and a few scraps of paper the room was totally empty.

6

Past and Present

'You've wasted more than enough of my valuable time,' said P.C. Brock as he dropped the children off outside Thornley Police Station, 'but I have just one more thing to say to you—'

The four children stood in silence, their heads bowed in shame, not daring to offer an explanation as to where the stolen goods had disappeared.

'—you keep out of dangerous old buildings,' continued the policeman. 'You're going to end up in Thornley Hospital if you play about in places like that. Now off you go home and no more silly pranks like this morning's episode!'

'I don't understand it,' said Michael as P.C. Brock stormed off into the police station. 'We all saw those things stored in the projection room, surely it wasn't some sort of ghostly mirage?'

'Of course it wasn't a mirage,' said Jenny scornfully. 'It's perfectly obvious that the boxes have been moved; somebody must have tipped them off.'

'I'm afraid she's right,' said Sparky. 'Benji probably warned them that we were about to fetch the police. Did you notice how quickly Benji vanished when we mentioned that the police would be involved? Tramps are very suspicious of the law and he probably had some arrangement with Moggy that if there were any danger he would let them know.'

'Well, all this has made us look right idiots,' said Stuart. 'Wait till my parents get to hear I've been inside an old building ready for demolition—my dad will demolish me!'

'I'm sure we missed something,' said Sparky thoughtfully. 'That P.C. Brock was so annoyed he didn't even examine the room properly. He would have found a clue if he'd been patient enough. I can sense that we missed something.'

'The only thing I missed was a good lie in,' said Michael. 'I've had quite enough of your "senses" for one day, I'm going home to sense my dinner. I'll see you at school on Monday.'

'Me too,' said Jenny. 'I'll see you on Monday.'

Stuart and Sparky walked home together. Sparky was very subdued and he didn't race off at his usual pace. Stuart knew that his brain was hard at work and he didn't interrupt him with trivial conversation. When they reached the corner shop at Royal Street Stuart said: 'Monday, then?'

'Er . . . yes,' replied Sparky, one hand on his glasses, and he crossed the road and walked off in the direction of Weaver Street.

In the playground on Monday morning Spike came straight up to Sparky and gripped him by his loose red jumper. He looked straight into Sparky's face and said: 'Moggy warned you to mind your own business, Carrot.

70

We've heard you've been sticking your nose into our affairs and my friends are going to teach you a lesson.'

While he was speaking Sparky was absolutely helpless and all he was aware of was a vile piece of pink bubble gum that rolled around Spike's mouth as he delivered his threat. Spike finished by pushing Sparky roughly away and spitting out his bubble gum onto the floor.

'He's disgusting,' said Jenny as she and Michael came across to check that Sparky had not been hurt.

'It's ridiculous,' complained Stuart joining them. 'We know very well that Spike, Moggy and their horrible spotty friend have committed these robberies yet we can't prove anything. Perhaps we should talk to Wacky Watson or get in touch with P.C. Short. We can't let them get away with it.'

'I think we can prove something,' said Sparky, straightening out his jumper. 'I think I know what it is we missed.'

'Well save it till later,' said Stuart. 'The bell is about to go and I've got to go and hand my football kit in before I go up to class.'

That afternoon Wacky Watson had a surprise in store for his fourth year junior class. The children knew that they would be working on their history project but instead of splitting them into groups as he usually did Mr Watson announced that they were to have a guest speaker and he arranged the chairs in rows facing the front of the class. At precisely two o'clock Mr Boyling

71

led a frail-looking gentleman into the classroom. It was obvious that the old man had very bad eyesight for he wore dark glasses and had to be helped into a chair at the front of the class.

'Right,' said Wacky Watson after a few words of thanks to Mr Boyling. 'I would like to introduce you to Mr Ernest Porter who has lived and worked in Thornley all his life. I'm sure Mr Porter won't mind me telling you that he is now seventy-four years old. Mr Porter has been an active member of the Local History Society for many years and I've asked him to come along this afternoon to talk about the war years. I'm sure Mr Porter will be willing to answer any questions you may have a little later, but for the time being I hope you are going to give him your full attention.'

Wacky Watson sat down behind his desk as the silver-haired old man rose rather unsteadily to his feet.

'Well, children,' began Mr Porter, 'I suppose the war years seem unreal to you, but to me they bring back vivid memories. I was just twenty-eight years old when war broke out . . . .'

Mr Porter soon had the children spellbound by his recollections of the war years. As the story of his life unwound the children discovered that he had not been able to serve in the army as his eyesight had not been up to the required standard. He had worked on the railways from the age of fourteen and at the outbreak of war he had become an air raid warden. It was his job to ensure that everywhere was completely blacked out when the siren sounded. He told the children how shutters had to be fitted to the windows and how shelters had been dug out in the grounds of St. Gregory's Church for the school children to use in an emergency. He spoke for nearly fifty minutes without a single interruption, feeding the children facts and information delicately embroidered with personal memories and reminiscences and then he lowered himself back down onto his chair to await any questions.

He did not have to wait long, for several children were eager to delve into his store of memories. Emma Wilkinson wanted to know what it was like inside an Anderson shelter and Peter Shields requested more information about the gas-masks that were issued to everyone. Wacky Watson had to choose the children to ask questions as Mr Porter was unable to see them clearly and it was not long before Michael was selected.

'Could you tell us about the night the ammunition train was hit?' asked Michael. 'We've been reading about it in an old edition of the *Thornley Chronicle.*'

'I can tell you about that night,' he said, slowly and deliberately. 'It was a Monday night—September 4th, 1940, and the sky was as black as pitch. They used to sound the siren from the hill at the top of the Parish Mill Fields and I remember it starting to wail at about ten fifteen. It would begin with a low groan and then rise to a constant, deafening pitch—the sound alone was enough to turn your blood cold. In some of the mills and factories the noise from the machinery meant that the siren couldn't be heard and it was the job of the A.R.P. to go round with rattles, like great loud football rattles they were. As soon as the warning was sounded it was lights off everywhere.

'The first wave of bombers came over almost immediately but there wasn't a single light showing in the whole of Thornley and they passed over us towards Manchester. We weren't so lucky with the next wave. The old Palace Theatre went first, and of course, the fire lit up the surrounding area. We still don't know if it was pure luck, but one of the bombers scored a direct hit on the ammunition train as it waited on Thornley railway bridge. It was as if the whole of Thornley had exploded; the whole town shook as explosion after explosion ripped through the waggons.'

Mr Porter paused for a moment as if remembering the terrible order of events. Stuart looked at Sparky, who had been sitting quite passively until the old man had begun his detailed description of the air raid. Now Stuart noticed that Sparky was sweating again and his eyes looked hazy, as if he were looking at Mr Porter but not really seeing him. Stuart wondered whether to attract Wacky's attention, but before he could make up his mind, Mr Porter started to speak again.

'I was amongst the first group of rescue workers to arrive at the station. The place was completely . . . .'

'Devastated,' broke in a voice from Stuart's table. Mr Porter paused. He couldn't see who it was that had spoken. but he leaned his head to one side as if to

74

listen intently.

The voice continued, rather slowly, the sentences sometimes vague and broken.

'They couldn't get to what was left of the train . . . rescue workers were everywhere. And the fire brigade trying to get out along the line . . . part of the bridge had been blown away and the train was still burning. People were screaming in the station . . . and the casualties, cut by flying glass . . . on the floor in the waiting room till the ambulances came. No lights, you see—the bombs were still dropping.'

Wacky Watson rose from his seat and walked towards Sparky who, ignoring everyone, continued to talk as if he was looking at a film of the disaster. Wacky stood directly in front of him and when there was still no sign of recognition he put a hand on Sparky's shoulder and said: 'Simon—are you all right? Do you feel quite well?'

The touch of the teacher's hand brought Sparky suddenly back to his senses and with a shiver of recognition he said: 'Sorry, sir, what did you say?'

'That was absolutely remarkable!' interrupted Mr Porter from the front of the class. 'That boy captured the scene perfectly. You must tell me where he got his information from.'

Sparky still appeared to be a little dazed and he looked around the room as if to remind himself where he was.

'You've done it again,' whispered Stuart. 'You cut in on Mr Porter and told us all about the ammunition train.'

Michael leaned across towards Stuart and pointing at

Sparky he whispered: 'He's a nutcase, he is. I've been telling you that ever since he came here.'

Wacky Watson invited the class to ask a few more questions and the rest of the lesson continued without further incident. By the time Mr Porter had been thanked and helped on his way it was afternoon break, and as they made their way down to the playground Stuart took the opportunity of asking a few questions of his own.

'Sparky,' he said, trying to sound as matter-of-fact as possible, 'how did you get to know all those details about the ammunition train?'

Sparky seemed immediately uneasy. He removed his glasses and began to clean them on his sleeve.

'I've told you,' he said, 'I've got a good memory for facts. A great deal of that information was in the old newspapers if you bother to look.'

'Oh, I will bother to look,' said Stuart, not being put off by Sparky's abrupt answer. 'But all that description—it was like listening to a news report. And you still haven't explained how you knew where to find Moggy's store—you didn't read about that in the newspaper.'

The children had just passed through the door into the playground and with a sigh of relief Sparky looked towards the gate and said: 'I think we've got a visitor.'

Stuart followed his gaze to see the familiar figure of P.C. Short striding across the playground, the younger children flocking towards him, eager to attract his attention.

Spike, who was chewing as usual, eyed the policeman coldly and then turned and walked away, pushing a little girl out of his path as he did so.

'Just the two I want to see,' said the big policeman, stopping in front of Stuart and Sparky. 'Perhaps we could step into the hall for a few minutes.'

P.C. Short opened the outside door for the children to step in before him.

'Now then,' he began, 'you two young gentlemen seem to have been getting yourselves into a spot of bother lately. Firstly we had that incident with those thugs the other evening and now my colleague P.C. Brock tells me you led him a right dance on Saturday morning. What have you got to say for yourselves?'

Stuart looked down at the floor and said nothing, ashamed at being questioned at all by the policeman, but Sparky pushed his glasses a little further onto his nose and after considering what the policeman said for a few moments he replied: 'Not quite right, I'm afraid. You see, the other evening we were innocent victims, and on Saturday morning we were unlucky.'

P.C. George Short looked extremely puzzled, and frowning deeply he said: 'Would you like to explain what you mean by unlucky?'

'Well,' began Sparky, thrusting his hands deep into the pockets of his maroon trousers, 'when we first broke into the Ritz, after we discovered that Bailey's ghost was really a tramp, and after we had inspected Benji's quarters, the stolen goods were in the projection room,

78

but when we returned with your colleague—who I must say was not very understanding—Benji had disappeared and there was nothing in the projection room.'

Sparky nodded with satisfaction, but poor P.C. Short looked even more puzzled than before.

'I suggest,' he said, doing his best to sound severe, 'that you keep well away from nasty thugs and dangerous old buildings. Do I make myself quite clear?'

'Absolutely,' said Sparky. 'And very good advice if I may say so!'

George Short shook his head, replaced his helmet, turned and walked out of the hall and back across the playground, the young children dancing around him again.

Stuart and Sparky had no sooner gone back out into the playground than Spike was there grabbing Sparky by his jumper, which was getting more and more misshapen.

'If you've told that copper anything Moggy will have you for dinner,' said Spike, and he let go of Sparky and pushed him away.

As Spike walked off across the playground, Sparky turned to Stuart and straightening his jumper he said: 'I know we've missed something, Stuart. We've got to go back to the old Ritz—we can prove Moggy and his gang have been in that projection room.'

Sparky pushed his glasses up again and produced a huge smile for Stuart's benefit. Stuart just stared back at him in disbelief.

'Sparky—you heard what P.C. Short said—we'd be

79

crazy to go back to the cinema. There's nothing there, Sparky.'

'I think you're wrong,' said Sparky still smiling, 'and when we go back this evening I'll prove it.'

'If you go back in that cinema,' said Stuart firmly, 'you go back on your own. I'm not coming with you this time, Sparky, and that's final!'

7

Trapped

Of all the qualities Sparky had, the one that Stuart found the most annoying was his quality of persuasion. He could always seem to talk Stuart round, probably because his arguments always sounded so convincing. By the time school had finished that day Sparky had already arranged for Stuart to meet him at six o'clock by the corner shop on Royal Street in order to find Sparky's 'proof' in the old cinema.

'I must be mad,' said Stuart as he made his way across the playground with Jenny and Michael after lessons had finished. Sparky had gone off to the library to change his book. He seemed to get through about four books a week on all sorts of different subjects.

'You are mad if you go back in that cinema,' said Michael. 'It's hanging around with Sparky that does it—he's gradually turning all his friends into nutcases like himself.'

'Stop being so nasty,' said Jenny thumping Michael with her school bag. 'I do agree with one thing though—if you go back to the Classic you must be mad.'

'But if I don't go,' protested Stuart, 'Moggy and his friends may never be caught. They could get away with it forever.'

'And if you do go,' said Michael, 'you might get caught and get yourself into a lot of trouble.'

81

'I think I'll have to take the chance,' said Stuart. 'I can't let Sparky go in there on his own.'

'I don't see why he has to be so mysterious about everything,' said Jenny, swinging her school bag backwards and forwards. 'He says he can prove Spike and his friends have been in the cinema and used that projection room, yet he won't tell us how he can prove it. And anyway, if the stuff isn't stored there any more what's the point of returning?'

'You know what Sparky's like,' replied Stuart, determined not to go back on his decision. 'He'll probably be able to work out where it's been moved to.'

'Well, it's your funeral,' said Michael, resigned to the fact that Stuart was not going to change his mind, 'but you're on your own this time. I'm not going near that place again. I'm still not convinced that Bailey's ghost doesn't exist; and how do you explain Benji's disappearance and all those boxes vanishing so quickly? Spirited away—I'm certain of it!'

'That's a lot of rubbish,' said Jenny, 'but you really are on your own because I'm not going back there either. You heard what P.C. Brock said; I don't want the police coming round to my house, my parents would go mad.'

'All right,' said Stuart, inwardly annoyed that his friends were deserting him, 'but just remember, we'll take all the credit when Moggy and his friends are caught.'

'If you manage to prove anything that leads to those three being caught you deserve to take all the credit,'

82

said Michael, 'but I think you're wasting your time.'

'I'll tell you what you can do,' said Stuart, prodding Michael with his finger, 'if I'm not in school tomorrow morning you can give the police a ring and tell them Bailey's ghost has got me!'

And he walked off down the road leaving Michael muttering about ghosts and spirits and Jenny still swinging her school bag.

There had been a change in the weather. The clear blue sky had gradually become patched with grey and now, as Stuart stood against the side wall of the corner shop on Royal Street, a light drizzle was beginning to fall. It was ten minutes past six and there was no sign of Sparky. Stuart was beginning to think that he wasn't going to turn up, and he was on the point of returning home when he spotted a red anorak hurrying down the street towards him.

'Where have you been?' demanded Stuart as Sparky stopped to catch his breath. 'I thought you weren't coming.'

'Sorry,' said Sparky, removing his glasses and wiping the spots of rain from the lenses. 'I went back for my anorak when the rain started.'

'Well never mind,' said Stuart, eager to be on the move. 'Let's get this over with, shall we?'

The two boys set off once again through the back streets of Thornley. The journey seemed to take longer than it had done on the previous Saturday morning, and the drizzle made everywhere seem drab and grey, particularly when they reached the demolition area. The boys walked in silence, for Stuart was secretly annoyed that he hadn't been told what they could expect to find in the old cinema, and as they passed the heaps of rubble that had once been streets and houses, he became more annoyed because Sparky hadn't realised that he was annoyed in the first place. By the time they reached the remains of Oak Street he could contain his anger no longer and he snapped: 'I hope this is going to be worthwhile!'

'Oh, I'm sure it will be very interesting,' replied Sparky, completely unaware that anything was wrong.

'Would you mind telling me . . . .'

'What it is I hope to find?' completed Sparky, heading for the fire exit around the back of the old cinema. 'I hope to find some sort of clue that will trap Moggy, Spike and their spotty friend, it's as simple as that.'

'I wish you wouldn't finish people's sentences for them,' said Stuart, and he thrust his hands deep into his pockets.

They reached the fire exit, the drizzle still falling, and they made their way carefully down the six stone steps which had become quite slippery now that they were wet. The doors at the bottom had been pulled closed but they gave way easily as soon as Sparky leaned on them.

'I've got a light,' he said, and from his anorak pocket he produced a small hand torch—the sort that people sometimes keep in the glove compartment of a car.

Sparky switched it on and it seemed to make hardly any impression as it shone into the dark corridor.

'That's tremendous,' said Stuart sarcastically.

'Well it's better than nothing,' said Sparky.

'Only just,' replied Stuart, and they made their way along the short corridor towards the main room of the cinema.

Stuart noticed that the door leading into the auditorium, which had been battered and splintered, was now off its hinges altogether and they had to step over pieces of it to enter the vast hall. It was obvious that somebody had visited the cinema since the children had left it with P.C. Brock the previous Saturday morning.

Inside the great room the darkness was intense. This time there were no shafts of spring sunshine to bring rays of comfort, and there was no one on guard outside to give a warning if danger approached. As he stood before the great white screen with its tattered curtains clutching his pathetic little light, Sparky gave a violent shiver which seemed to travel through the cold air until it reached Stuart who shivered in response.

'It seems worse this time,' said Stuart in a whisper, his eyes trying to search the darkness.

Sparky could easily understand what Stuart meant. On this chill Monday evening there was nothing to remind the boys of the reality of the outside world. It was as though their senses had been reduced to a minimum, yet even in this darkness their eyes gradually adjusted and they began to move slowly forward at the

85

bottom of the aisles, keeping level with the great screen.

For some unknown reason Sparky did not turn up the wide centre aisle that sloped towards the projection room. Instead, he continued to cross the cinema in front of the screen, intending to use the aisle on the far side. Stuart was close behind him and each time the boys took a step the wooden floorboards, soft and rotten through age, groaned and creaked under their weight.

. Just over halfway across the room Sparky had second thoughts and he stopped in his tracks, prodding at the floor with his foot.

'I think we've made a mistake,' he whispered. 'This floor seems a bit unsteady to say the least.'

He had no sooner spoken than the boards beneath their feet seemed to tremble and strain and there was a sudden almighty crack followed by the sound of splintering wood. Both boys instinctively let out a scream as they crashed through the floor and felt themselves falling through space before landing heavily amidst a pile of wood, bricks and rubble. The scream echoed back at them time and time again, confused with the crash of the breaking floor, and for a few brief moments neither Sparky nor Stuart was aware of what had happened. Sparky was coughing a hoarse, barking cough irritated by the cloud of dust that had been caused by the fall.

'Are you all right?' asked Stuart, still in a crumpled heap but slowly coming to his senses.

'I ... think so ... ' replied Sparky, coughing and spluttering in a most alarming manner. 'I've ... twisted an ankle, I think . . . and I can't find my glasses, but I think I'm all right. What about you?'

'I'm fine,' said Stuart, adjusting his position so that he crouched on all fours amongst the rubble. He still couldn't see Sparky properly, but he could make out Sparky's feeble light nearby and he crawled towards it.

'Can you sit up?' asked Stuart, concerned that Sparky might be more badly hurt than he was admitting.

'I am sitting up!' snapped Sparky as if to reassure him. 'We've fallen through the floor, you know.'

'I gathered that,' said Stuart. 'What are we going to do?'

'Well, we have to try and get out, of course,' said Sparky, as if it was the obvious answer to give.

Stuart shone the faint beam upwards and he could just make out the jagged edges of the broken floorboards some way above his head. Sparky was groping in the darkness for his glasses. He couldn't see a thing without them—in fact, he couldn't see too well even when he had them on. He found them amongst the rubble and although one arm was slightly bent the lenses were intact and he was able to put them back on his nose.

'We're never going to get up there without help,' said Stuart, peering upwards from his position on the rubble. He had crawled nearer to Sparky and he still spoke in a whisper although there seemed no reason to do so.

'I think we've got ourselves into a bit of a mess,' admitted Sparky.

'We can always try shouting for help,' suggested

Stuart.

'I don't think that would be a very good idea,' said Sparky, considering the suggestion carefully. 'The cinema would only shout back at us.'

Stuart knew that Sparky was referring to the echo that bounced back from the vast empty hall, but he did have a strange way of putting things.

'Have you got a better idea, then? You're the one who's supposed to be the bright spark. I certainly don't feel like sitting down here all night—we might be stuck here forever like Bailey's ghost!'

'I suggest,' said Sparky with great deliberation, 'that we take a look around underneath these floorboards. There could be another way out somewhere, some steps up to a cellar hatch, maybe.'

'I suppose we've got nothing to lose,' said Stuart, not at all confident that it would prove a worthwhile exercise.

The two boys stood up carefully and with their feet they pushed aside some of the debris that had fallen with them so that they could feel the firm concrete of the cellar floor beneath. Above their heads the wide hole gaped, the wood frayed and splintered at the edges. Stuart stretched upwards to arm's length but it was impossible to reach floor level no matter how he strained. He soon gave up and turning to Sparky he said: 'Let's take a look, then.'

The light from Sparky's torch was by no means good but it did help a little, and as the boys moved slowly away

from the hole they had created they were grateful for the feeble beam. It soon became obvious that it was going to be very difficult to move around at all, so intense was the darkness, but the boys persevered, shuffling forward a few steps at a time, Sparky with a hand on Stuart's shoulder for guidance.

They had not gone very far into the great cellar when Stuart stopped and in a voice that for the first time hinted of despair he said: 'This is hopeless, Sparky, we're wasting our time!'

'I think you may be right,' Sparky agreed, and he switched his light off for a minute to save the batteries. 'We're never going to find anything under here. Let's go back towards the opening.'

The boys slowly edged their way back until they were beside the rubble again, beneath the hole in the floor. They sat down close to each other not knowing what to try next, neither of them bothering to speak. After a while Stuart nudged Sparky with his elbow and said: 'I suppose this is what it must have been like in an Anderson shelter—cold, dark and boring.'

Sparky didn't answer for a minute. He was considering Stuart's statement carefully. Eventually he said: 'Yes, I think you're right, Stuart. It was definitely very boring, especially once the novelty had worn off, but it was also a lot more cramped in an Anderson shelter than it is down here, and of course, if there was an air raid taking place it was very noisy, as you can imagine.'

'Yes, I can imagine,' said Stuart, 'but you always seem

90

to talk about the war as if . . . .'

'Oh, I know what I'm talking about,' said Sparky brusquely. 'I assure you I know what I'm talking about.'

Stuart was about to continue the conversation when he suddenly became alert. He stiffened in the darkness, and nudging Sparky again he whispered: 'Listen!'

There was a pause and then Sparky said: 'Listen to what?'

'I don't know exactly—just listen!'

Sparky took his glasses off in the darkness and inclined his head to one side.

'I think I can hear it,' he said. 'What is it?'

'I don't know,' replied Stuart. 'I thought it was you scratching in the rubble at first.'

'It's not me,' replied Sparky indignantly, 'but I agree, it does sound like scratching and it seems to be getting closer, down here in the cellar.'

'Put your light back on,' said Stuart. 'See if you can make anything out.'

Sparky replaced his glasses and then switched on his torch, shining the faint beam directly in front of him. The two boys strained their eyes into the darkness, following the path of the beam, but they could see nothing. Yet the scratching sound seemed to be growing louder, coming closer as the boys sat huddled together on the rubble. Then suddenly Stuart let out a terrific yell which pierced the darkness and sent Sparky reeling sideways clutching his ears. When the echo died away Sparky shouted: 'Stuart—what's the matter, Stuart?'

'It's touching me,' screamed Stuart clutching Sparky's arm. 'I can feel it against my legs!'

8

Sparky's Proof

For a moment Sparky seemed confused and for once he didn't know what to do.

'Shine your light down,' shouted Stuart. 'I can still feel something at my feet.'

Sparky directed the light towards Stuart's feet and the two boys recoiled as it picked out the clear form of a large brown rat, frozen like a statue as the light affected it, its eyes wide and staring, and then moving, scurrying off into the darkness. Then there was another one crossing in front of them, and Sparky felt another brush against his legs, and the whole area of rubble around their feet seemed to come alive as several more rats scurried by, some making a strange squeaking noise.

The movement had its effect on the boys, and their first reaction was one of panic. They leapt to their feet and stamped and shouted and kicked at the rubble to scare the creatures away, back into the underground darkness, and when they were sure that the rats were no longer near them Stuart sank down onto the rubble exhausted and said: 'We've got to get out of here, Sparky. It's like a nightmare. I feel as if I've been taking part in a horror film.'

'There is a way,' said Sparky, still breathless after the sudden excitement. 'What if we pile up the rubble as high as we can and then you get up on my shoulders?

You might be able to pull yourself up through the hole.'

Stuart looked up at the gaping hole with the boards broken and splintered and he said doubtfully: 'I suppose it's worth a try, but I can't really see those boards taking my weight.'

'We've got nothing to lose,' said Sparky, pushing his glasses back. 'Unless you want to just sit here and wait for the rats to come back. What do you say?'

'What are we waiting for?' replied Stuart as he rose to his feet and began piling together the wood and the rubble that had crashed through the floor with him.

It was not easy to build up the debris into any sort of decent mound, for the pieces were small and there wasn't really that much material to work with. After about ten minutes of scraping and gathering the boys ended up with no more than a small bump on the concrete floor, but it did take them that bit nearer to the hole when they stood on it.

'Right,' said Stuart, looking up at the edge of the hole. 'Are you sure you can take my weight if I climb on your shoulders?'

'Of course I can,' said Sparky indignantly.

'Here goes then!'

Sparky crouched down on the rubble, his hands slightly forward to steady himself, and Stuart climbed onto his shoulders, putting his legs astride Sparky's head.

'Mind my glasses,' protested Sparky. 'Keep your big knees out of my ears.'

'Can you stand up?' asked Stuart, ignoring the comments.

'I'll try,' replied Sparky, and he slowly wobbled to his feet groaning under Stuart's weight, his face even redder than usual with the strain.

'Great,' said Stuart, 'I can reach the boards. Just take one step to the right so that I can get a good grip.'

Sparky tottered sideways, just managing to keep his balance.

'That will do nicely,' said Stuart. 'I've got my hands over the boards and the wood doesn't feel too bad. I'm going to try and haul myself out—here goes.'

Stuart transferred all his weight onto the remains of the wooden boards. He groaned with effort as he struggled to pull himself over the edge, and for a brief moment his legs dangled in space as he hauled himself clear of Sparky's shoulders. Sparky glanced up just in time to see Stuart drag one leg over the edge of the boards and he was about to congratulate his friend when there was a tremendous crack as once again the rotten boards gave way and Stuart crashed back down on top of Sparky in a great mess of splintered wood.

The boys picked themselves from the floor, the cloud of dust causing Sparky to gasp for air.

'I was nearly there,' said Stuart in frustration. 'We've got to give it....'

'One more go,' finished Sparky, coughing and spluttering as he repositioned his glasses on his nose. 'Yes, I quite agree—let's try again, shall we?'

95

'At least we've got a bit more rubble to build up,' said Stuart, doing his best to sound optimistic.

The boys set to work rebuilding their mound and in no time at all they were ready to try again.

'Perhaps you'd be better on my shoulders,' suggested Stuart. 'I think you might be a little lighter than me.'

'The problem is,' said Sparky, scratching his head thoughtfully, 'I can't see what I'm doing! I suggest you have another go—you nearly made it last time.'

Stuart pulled himself up onto Sparky's bony shoulders and Sparky rose unsteadily to his feet again. This time they had positioned themselves correctly first time and Stuart was able to get a good grip on what remained of the wooden boards. He pulled with all his might and with one swift jerk he found himself lying flat on the wooden floor of the cinema hall. He rolled away from the edge of the hole, frightened that the boards would give way beneath him again, and he stood up carefully and shouted: 'I've made it, Sparky! I've made it!'

'What about me?' enquired a feeble voice from somewhere beneath his feet. 'How can I get out?'

'Wait a minute,' said Stuart, and he looked around the great hall for something he could use. It was still dark, but compared to the darkness beneath the floor Stuart found he was able to see quite clearly. His eyes settled on the remains of the tattered screen curtains hanging limply from their broken frames, and Stuart knew he had found the answer. He edged away from the hole and made his way towards the corner of the screen. Grab-

bing hold of part of the old velvet curtain he jerked it downwards. Stuart expected a struggle but a huge section of the curtain tore away and dropped at his feet. Stuart gathered it together and dragged it back towards the hole in the floor. He spread it out and then folded it double to strengthen it. Passing one end through the metal legs of a nearby cinema seat, he dropped the other end through the floor and down to Sparky.

'How about that,' he shouted. 'Can you climb up, do you think?'

'That's great,' replied Sparky from beneath the floor. 'If you can hold it steady I'll be up in no time.'

Stuart sat down and wedged his feet against the metal seat. He took the curtain around his back and gripped it firmly.

'Ready when you are!' he shouted.

Stuart felt the material tighten as Sparky began to lift himself from the hole. There were a few strange grunting noises and at one point there was a sharp tearing sound from the curtain, but Stuart soon felt the material slacken as Sparky pulled himself clear of the hole.

'That's a relief,' said Sparky as he sank down by Stuart in one of the few remaining cinema seats that were still intact. The effort had quite exhausted Sparky and his face seemed to glow redder than ever in the dimness of the cinema hall.

'You look like a traffic light that's permanently on stop,' commented Stuart.

'I must admit, I feel a bit flushed after that,' said Sparky. 'Still, now we can get on with the job we came to do.'

Stuart had quite forgotten that they had entered the cinema with a purpose and he was not all all keen to remain in the place, especially as he had lost track of the time and was not expected to be home late.

'Don't you think we should forget all about this business?' asked Stuart hopefully, knowing full well the answer he would receive.

'Of course not,' replied Sparky. 'You follow me and we'll soon be done in here.'

Sparky made his way carefully along the row of battered seats, occasionally testing the floor with his front foot before putting his full weight on it. Stuart followed him growing more and more impatient, wondering if Michael's opinion of Sparky bore some truth after all.

When he reached the end of the row Sparky turned up the centre aisle and proceeded with more confidence towards the projection room. He stopped when he came to the solid door and turning to his friend he said: 'I think we should take another look in here.'

The two boys pulled at the heavy door which creaked slowly open. Sparky peered inside, his head moving first to the left and then scanning the room carefully, taking everything in.

'As I thought,' he announced, 'it's empty!'

'Have you brought me all this way to show me an

empty room?' demanded Stuart. 'You didn't really think they'd move all the stuff back in, did you?'

'No, no, of course not,' said Sparky. 'This is just what I expected. But let's take a closer look inside, shall we—you never know.'

Sparky stepped into the small, square room and Stuart followed him, wondering what on earth it was they were supposed to be looking for. There was no window in the projection room, only the small opening from which the films had been shown, but with the door wide open light filtered in from the foyer. The battered cardboard box was still on the floor as it had been the previous Saturday, so were the few scraps of paper, but as far as Stuart could see there was nothing else of interest. Sparky walked up to the box and peered down at it. He moved it with his foot and then flicked it over and peered at it again, keeping one hand on his glasses in case they fell off his nose. He picked the box up and looked inside before replacing it carefully on the floor.

'Nothing there,' muttered Sparky, more to himself than to Stuart; he looked around again and then moved a few paces towards the scraps of paper.

Sparky repeated the process, staring down at the bits of brown wrapping paper that had been discarded on the floor, poking at them with his foot, picking them up and examining them closely and then deciding that they were of no interest to him.

'That is disappointing,' said Sparky. 'Very disappointing.'

All this time Stuart had been standing in the doorway growing more and more impatient.

'Would you mind telling me what you expected to find?' he demanded. 'We've been stuck in this place for ages and all we've managed to do is fall through the floor and find an empty box!'

'Well, I have to admit, I'm disappointed,' repeated Sparky. 'Very disappointed. I thought there might have been a label or something on the box that could have identified where it came from, but there's nothing—it's just an empty box as you can see.'

'Well, now that you're satisfied,' said Stuart, 'do you think we could go home, please?'

'Yes, I suppose we had better make a move,' said Sparky, and he began to move towards the door. He had only taken two steps when he stopped, a strange expression suddenly appearing on his face.

'What's the matter now?' asked Stuart in disbelief.

'I think it's on my shoe,' replied Sparky, and he looked down at his right foot.

'Why do you always have to talk in riddles? What do you mean it's on your shoe?'

'The answer,' replied Sparky, his voice rising with excitement. 'The proof—it's on my shoe!'

Stuart took a step towards him and bent forward slightly to take a closer look at Sparky's shoe, and there, stuck firmly to the end of his foot was a huge blob of pink bubble gum.

'It's Spike's gum,' said Stuart, his eyes opening wide as

he realised what Sparky was getting at.

'Exactly!' announced Sparky in triumph. 'And if Spike's gum is here that means that Spike must have been here with it, wouldn't you agree? P.C. Short knows that Spike is always chewing the horrible stuff—he had it stuck to his trousers if you remember.'

'Yes, but it still doesn't prove that he had anything to do with the robberies, does it?' said Stuart. 'It just proves he has been in the cinema.'

Sparky thought for a moment, taking his glasses off and rubbing the lenses on his sleeve before replying. 'I'm afraid it's as much as we're going to get,' he said. 'I reckon if P.C. Short were to have a little chat with Spike, tell him that some real evidence had been found, Spike would admit everything. It's just a matter of applying pressure, bluffing if you like.'

'So what do we do now?' asked Stuart, still staring down at the gum that Sparky hadn't bothered to remove from his shoe.

'It's back to the police station, I'm afraid,' said Sparky replacing his glasses. 'And the sooner we get there the better. Let's make a move, shall we?'

In his eagerness to get away Sparky pushed past Stuart and disappeared out of the projection room. Stuart shook his head and turned to follow him, wondering what on earth the police would make of a piece of pink bubble gum stuck on the end of Sparky's foot. Stuart took one last look around the small, square room and then hurried to catch up with Sparky. He didn't have far to go, for as soon as he passed through the doorway he walked straight into the back of Sparky who had stopped in his tracks.

'What are you playing at now?' protested Stuart. 'I thought you were in a hurry?'

Sparky made no effort to answer, he just raised his arm and pointed straight ahead. Stuart stared past him towards the vast hall of the cinema. The light from the foyer was behind them, and as the boys gazed in silence, a black figure was clearly visible not more than five metres away, standing perfectly still, staring straight ahead in the direction of the two boys.

'What do we do?' whispered Stuart nervously. 'Shall we make a run for it?'

'I don't think so,' replied Sparky, his voice quite steady and confident. 'I think this could be just the bit of good luck we've been waiting for!'

9

A Convincing Story

The dark figure took a few hesitant steps towards the boys and then stopped, unsure whether or not it was wise to advance further. Sparky stood his ground, facing the black outline with confidence, and when he saw that it had checked its advance he said in a clear, loud voice: 'Come on, Benji, nobody's going to harm you. You can trust us, you know.'

'Is that right, now?' replied the tramp suspiciously. 'I can trust you, can I, when you go and fetch the police into my quarters and force me out of my own home.'

Stuart sighed with relief when he recognised the familiar voice and turning to Sparky he said: 'How did you know it was Benji? How could you tell from that distance? He just appeared as a black shape to me. I thought your eyesight was bad?'

Sparky didn't bother to answer Stuart but continued to address the tramp.

'It wasn't us who drove you out, Benji. You warned Moggy and his friends, didn't you? I hope they paid you well for your services?'

'They didn't give me anything,' said Benji as he joined the boys outside the projection room. 'They promised me all sorts, but they didn't give me a thing. They're a bad lot—you mark my words.'

'We know very well that they're a bad lot,' said Stuart.

'That's why we tried to do something about it, but you helped them get away.'

'I've told you,' said Benji getting irritated, 'they promised to pay me. They said there would be money for food and things to make my quarters more comfortable. I wasn't to know they'd cheat on me, was I?'

'What are you doing back here?' asked Stuart. 'Why have you returned?'

'It's my home,' explained Benji quietly. 'The council will be knocking it down soon—progress they call it—I want to spend a few more months in the old place before it disappears completely.'

'Listen, Benji,' said Sparky scratching his head as a new idea occurred to him. 'Those three bullies cheated you. They used you for their own rotten ends. Why don't you help us put them where they belong? Why don't you get even with them?'

Benji sniffed and wiped his nose on the sleeve of his coat. He shuffled past the boys towards the cinema foyer, towards his beloved quarters, then turning to face them he said firmly: 'I want nothing to do with no police, and that's final!' And he disappeared down the short flight of steps leaving the two boys staring after him, Sparky still with the blob of pink gum stuck to his shoe.

'Well we can't . . . .'

'Make him help us?' completed Sparky. 'Oh, I think we should be able to persuade him. If we can get Benji to talk to the police Moggy, Spike and their horrible spotty friend won't stand a chance. Let's give it a try, shall we?'

Sparky set off down the few steps in pursuit of Benji, and Stuart followed close behind. It suddenly occurred to Stuart that since this strange, red boy had arrived in Thornley he had spent most of his spare time following him around.

Benji had gone into the small storeroom behind the sweet counter and was sitting on one of his wooden boxes pretending to look at an old newspaper. When Sparky and Stuart entered the room he continued to scan the paper, ignoring them completely. Sparky noticed that he was wearing an expensive-looking digital wrist watch, and walking up to the tramp he said: 'That's a nice watch you have, Benji. I wonder if you could tell me the time, please? We seem to have been in this building for hours.'

Benji glared at Sparky and then glancing down at his wrist he said sharply: 'It's seven o'clock—time you went home.'

Stuart was surprised it was not much later. He had expected to have to explain to his parents why he was out so late.

'I suppose you have bought that watch recently,' continued Sparky. 'It looks brand new, you see.'

Benji put his paper to one side and pulled his sleeve down over the watch as if to protect it.

'It's none of your business where I got it from, see? I've got it, and that's all that concerns you.'

'But it isn't your watch, is it, Benji? You got it from

106

the projection room, didn't you?'

'What if I did?' snapped the tramp, looking more and more uncomfortable. 'They owed me, see? You said yourself they cheated me. Anyway, they're not going to miss one little watch from the haul they've got, are they?'

Sparky came a little closer to the tramp and pulling up the remaining wooden box he sat down near him.

'No, they probably won't miss the watch,' said Sparky, 'but the point is, it isn't their watch in the first place—they stole it from somebody else.'

Stuart watched from the doorway, fascinated by the way Sparky was working on the tramp. Benji didn't know what to say, he just sat there twitching his fingers and pulling nervously at his woollen hat. Finally he said: 'You wouldn't tell the police, would you? You wouldn't inform on poor old Benji?'

'Not if you help us,' said Sparky jumping to his feet again. 'You've got to help us catch those three louts. Remember—they've done you no favours. It was their fault you had to leave your quarters.'

Benji thought for a moment, his fingers twitching more than ever, and then suddenly he seemed to make up his mind and he said: 'All right, I'll help you! But what about the watch? I don't want to be caught in possession of stolen property.'

'That's no problem,' said Stuart, finally joining in the conversation. 'We can say that they left it behind in the projection room when they were in such a hurry to

107

move the stolen goods. You just wish to return it to its rightful owner.'

Benji nodded his head in satisfaction. His fingers had stopped twitching and he even appeared to have something near to a smile on his stubbly face.

'What do we do next?' he asked, eager to be helpful now that he had made up his mind.

'Well, I think the first thing you should do is tell us where it is Moggy and his friends have moved their haul,' said Stuart.

'That's easy,' said Benji, beginning to enjoy himself. 'It's not so far away from here. Well, they wouldn't have had time to move it far, would they? They had to find somewhere similar to this cinema, somewhere not being used, I mean. They took the stuff away in boxes and they've hidden it . . . .'

'In the old railway station,' completed Sparky quietly. 'They've hidden it in the waiting room, haven't they? Nobody goes in there any more—the whole station has been boarded up for years.'

Benji's mouth had dropped open in sheer astonishment. In fact, he was so amazed that his fingers had begun twitching again.

'How on earth did he know that?' said Benji, addressing Stuart. 'He couldn't have possibly known where they'd moved to—I only knew myself because I followed them there!'

Stuart had long since ceased to be surprised at anything Sparky either said or did, and in an attempt to put Benji at ease again he explained calmly: 'Sparky just knows, it doesn't really matter how.'

'After all these years,' continued Sparky, a far away look in his eyes. 'Who would have thought—the old railway station after all these years.'

'I suggest we get to the police station,' said Stuart. 'It will be getting dusk in an hour or so and I've got to get home before it gets dark.'

Sparky shook his head abruptly as if to free himself from his thoughts, and securing his glasses on his nose he said: 'Yes, let's make a move, shall we? I'm sure the police will be keen to listen to us this time.'

The two children made their way quickly through the dark cinema, Benji shuffling behind them pulling at his hat and muttering every so often. They kept to the left aisle in the main hall, avoiding the rotten wood in front of the screen that had so nearly caused their downfall. As they left the hall and entered the short corridor that led to the fire exit Stuart glanced back at the gaping hole in the floor and shuddered as he thought of the rats brushing against him in their dark prison.

Once out in the open the children stopped for a moment and gulped in the fresh, spring air, glad to be away from the musty atmosphere that filled the old cinema. The drizzle had stopped and the clouds had cleared leaving a freshly washed blue sky. It was a perfect spring evening, warm for the end of April, and as they walked through the derelict streets Stuart thought that even the ruins held a certain attraction that he hadn't noticed before.

The boys did not take long to leave the ruined streets behind them. Sparky had set off at his usual lightning pace and Stuart had needed to remind him several times that Benji was getting left behind. The old tramp had to stop every so often to get his breath; this, together with a rasping, chesty cough suggested that he was not in the best of health and certainly not used to a brisk evening walk through the streets of Thornley.

When they eventually reached Thornley Police Station Benji stopped, looking most uncomfortable once again. Stuart guessed that he was having second thoughts and he went over to the tramp and took him by the arm.

'Come on, Benji—there's no going back now.'

The three visitors opened the door and entered the station. Stuart looked over to the counter and let out a low groan, for there, leaning on the counter writing in a small notebook was P.C. Brock.

'Just our luck,' muttered Stuart as they approached the stern-looking policeman.

P.C. Brock didn't bother to look up at first and Sparky coughed politely to attract his attention. The policeman raised his eyes slightly and stared at Sparky, then at Stuart before finally fixing his gaze on Benji, who by this time was extremely nervous. Before anyone could speak P.C. Brock said coldly: 'I hope you haven't come to bother me with another one of your fairy stories.'

Sparky's face immediately turned bright red. He

marched straight up to the counter and placing both hands on the flat surface he announced with confidence: 'We have some definite evidence that will lead you to the thieves and hopefully save the Thornley police from any further embarrassment.'

P.C. Brock took a deep breath and his face turned almost as red as Sparky's, so that the two of them faced each other like a couple of boiled beetroots. Benji looked absolutely horrified and took a step back towards the door.

'Evidence, is it?' said P.C. Brock, doing his best to remain calm. 'Perhaps you would like to show me this evidence.'

Sparky stared at him for a moment longer just to keep him in suspense, then he suddenly ducked out of sight below the counter, pulled his shoe off and reappeared to bang it down on the counter in front of the astonished policeman, the blob of pink gum somewhat grubby, but still stuck firmly to the end of the shoe.

P.C. Brock seemed to shake visibly with anger as he stared at Sparky's evidence, and Stuart decided that he had better say something before they were physically thrown out of the police station.

'If I could just explain,' he said, grabbing Sparky's arm and pulling him back from the counter. 'We have been back inside the old Classic and this piece of bubble gum was on the floor in the projection room.'

'You've been where?' said P.C. Brock slowly and deliberately, rising to his full height. 'You mean to say

111

that you've been back into that cinema after all my warnings?'

'We went back,' said Sparky, still angry at the reception they had received, 'because we knew you were wrong. And now we have proof because that is Spike's gum stuck on the end of my shoe, so what have you got to say to that?'

Poor P.C. Brock was looking more and more confused. He didn't really know what to say, and after a moment's consideration he announced: 'Wait here,' and he disappeared into the back of the police station. He emerged with P.C. George Short and several other policemen who were curious to see what all the fuss was about.

'Hello, you two,' said P.C. Short with a broad grin. 'What's all this I hear about tramps and chewing gum?'

Stuart gave a sigh of relief and began to explain clearly how they had gone back into the old cinema and found a piece of Spike's gum in the projection room. P.C. Short looked hard at the sticky mess on the end of Sparky's shoe and the other policemen gathered round the curious object, pointing at it and muttering with interest.

'It does stick to the most unusual places does that gum,' said P.C. Short, 'and I have to admit, I'm inclined to believe your story about Spike and his friends, but one piece of bubble gum doesn't prove that they are responsible for all the recent robberies. We'll need more to go on than a piece of bubble gum if we're to make it stick, so

112

to speak!'

'That's where Benji comes in,' said Sparky. 'He's got something that will give you all the proof you'll need.'

The policemen looked across to the feeble old tramp who pulled his woollen hat off and twitched nervously under their gaze.

'Come on then, Benji,' said P.C. Short kindly. 'Let's see what you've got for us, shall we?'

Benji took a hesitant step forward and removing the watch from his wrist he said: 'I didn't steal it, you know—they must have dropped it when they were in such a hurry to move the stuff.'

P.C. Short took the watch from Benji, taking care not to get too close to the tramp. He handed it to P.C. Brock and said: 'Check if it's on the list of missing property, will you?'

Brock disappeared with the watch into the back room. It wasn't long before he returned clutching a batch of papers which evidently gave details of all the items that had been stolen in the recent spate of burglaries.

'It's here,' he said, jabbing a finger at one of the pages. 'Comes from the vicarage they did a fortnight ago.'

'Right,' said P.C. Short turning to the boys. 'You've done well. Now we can go and question these friends of yours and see if we can recover the rest of the stolen property.'

'But that's what we've been trying to tell Sherlock Holmes here,' said Sparky, pointing a finger at an embarrassed P.C. Brock. 'We know where they've

113

moved their store to—it's all hidden away in the old railway station—in the waiting room if I'm not mistaken. We tried to tell P.C. Brock but he seems a little slow this evening!'

P.C. Brock coughed uncomfortably and lowered his eyes.

'Well I never!' said P.C. Short. 'What are we waiting for then—we'll get a couple of cars sorted out and go and take a look, shall we? You two boys had better come along as you seem to know exactly where to find everything.'

'Can I come too?' asked Benji, suddenly feeling a little more confident.

'You're not going anywhere, my friend, until you've had a good bath,' said P.C. Short looking at him with distaste. 'P.C. Brock—see what you can arrange, will you?'

'A bath . . .' protested Benji, clearly distressed at the thought of soap and water. 'I never have a bath . . . . I haven't had a bath for years . . . only dirty people have baths . . . . I had a wash last month . . . .'

But his protests were to no avail, for P.C. Brock took him firmly by the arm and led him away into the back room, still muttering, his woollen hat clutched between his twitching hands.

10

Sparky's Return

Within ten minutes Stuart and Sparky were speeding through the streets of Thornley in the back of a squad car. A second car followed close behind, its headlights piercing the gathering dusk.

'It feels unreal,' said Stuart. 'I'm sure I shouldn't be here—it's like a bad dream.'

'Don't worry, you'll wake up soon,' said Sparky unsympathetically. 'I've got a feeling we're going to find a little more than stolen goods when we arrive at the station.'

'Not another one of your feelings,' protested Stuart. 'I'm getting sick to death of your feelings.' And he sank a little further down in the back seat of the car.

Another few minutes saw the cars turning off the main road and down a small cobbled track that led to a car park at the side of the old station.

It was a part of the town that Stuart was not familiar with, for the railway station had been closed for as long as he could remember.

The car park was no more than a large stretch of rough ground and the passengers were jolted and jostled from side to side as the cars looked for a suitable parking space away from the huge puddles and other obstructions that littered the ground. To the right of the car park the land rose away steeply and was bounded by a

116

great stone wall. The station was to the left, and as the boys stepped from the car they looked down on it. Four policemen, including P.C. Short, had travelled with the children, and as they viewed the two platforms, the lines stretching away towards the great stone railway bridge, everywhere seemed quiet and peaceful.

Sparky stared down at the old station and for once Stuart thought he looked quite pale.

'How do we get down to the platform?' asked one of the policemen.

'You'd better ask this young man,' replied P.C. Short, nodding towards Sparky. 'He's obviously been here before as he knows where everything is.'

Stuart said nothing.

'Well the front entrance is round on the main road,' explained Sparky. 'I doubt if they will have used that—they would have been seen too easily. You'd better put one of your men there just in case, though.'

'You heard,' said P.C. Short, and one of the policemen made off across the car park towards the front of the station.

'There's a side gate over there,' continued Sparky, pointing to a large wooden gate set in what remained of the station fencing. 'I think you will find that will take us down to the platforms.'

'Right,' said P.C. Short, 'let's go and take a look, shall we?'

One of the remaining policemen stayed with the cars with an instruction to radio for help if he thought it

117

necessary. P.C. Short and his other colleague followed Stuart and Sparky to the station gate. Sparky pushed against it, but it was locked and bolted from the inside.

'It's locked,' announced Sparky turning to face the policemen.

'Well climb over it, lad—we're not going to tell you off this time. Besides, you two seem pretty good at getting into places where you're not supposed to be.'

Sparky hitched himself up to the top of the gate and then dropped down onto the other side. The others followed him, and they stood for a moment at the top of a great flight of stone steps that led down to a long platform.

'Go on, lad,' said P.C. Short, 'we're right behind you.'

The group descended the steps carefully, for some were cracked and broken and one had fallen away altogether. At the bottom of the steps was the first of two platforms, the station name still intact on a large maroon board. The station was silent, almost eerie in the fading evening light. The railway lines stretched away to the left, rusted and broken through lack of use. To the right, not far from the main entrance was a red brick building which had once served as the waiting room. A storage yard lay beyond the platforms and there were several old railway carriages standing, including a diesel engine that had leaked a huge pool of black, slimy oil which was slowly creeping its way along the track.

As they stood on the deserted platform Stuart suddenly thought of all the people from the past who must have stood shivering on the same spot, and of the ammunition train and the terrible night of the explosion, and he could sense that Sparky's thoughts were on the same subject. Stuart looked along the line towards the bridge and in his mind he pictured the supply train, stationary in the darkness, motionless before that last awful moment when the bomb fell. His thoughts were suddenly interrupted, for Sparky was on the move again, heading along the platform towards the waiting room.

Halfway along the platform Sparky stopped, frozen like a statue, staring straight ahead. Stuart couldn't see why he had stopped at first but when he looked past Sparky in the direction of the waiting room the reason was clear enough. Just to the right of the building, almost in the middle of the platform stood the familiar figure of Spike, absolutely still, frozen in a similar stance to Sparky so that the two of them stood facing each other like gunfighters before the big showdown.

P.C. Short was the first to make a move, and as soon as he took a step forward Spike was galvanised into action.

'It's the coppers!' he screamed. 'That carrot kid's fetched the coppers! Run for it, Moggy—make a run for it!'

The waiting room door suddenly burst open and Moggy leapt out onto the platform followed by his spotty friend.

'Split up!' yelled Moggy. 'There's only two coppers!'

Spike had already disappeared round the back of the

waiting room, and before making their move the two policemen watched for a minute to see which direction Moggy and his friend would take. Moggy jumped down onto the line and crossed quickly to the next platform. Beyond the platform was another line running parallel to the first. Moggy had worked out that if he was quick enough he could pass the policemen by making off down the line towards the railway bridge.

'I'll take him!' yelled P.C. Short, and he jumped down onto the track in pursuit of Moggy who had already gained a fair bit of ground.

The other policeman ran towards the spotty boy who was obviously less bright, for as yet he hadn't decided in which direction to make his escape. When he saw the policeman charging towards him he turned and ran for all he was worth towards the main entrance, forgetting that there was no possible way out as the doors had been firmly secured.

The policeman who had been left guarding the cars had a perfect view of the events being acted out beneath him, and seeing Moggy racing down the line towards the railway bridge he immediately radioed for assistance in the hope that his escape route could be blocked.

All this happened so quickly that Sparky was still stuck to the spot from which he had first sighted Spike. It was only when Spike sneaked out from behind the waiting room wall that his mind began to take in all that was happening. He watched for a moment as Spike crawled on all fours to the edge of the track and lowered

himself down onto the line. Spike had spotted the disused railway carriages in the storage yard beyond the platforms and he was moving steadily in that direction.

'Stuart, let's follow him,' shouted Sparky, jumping down onto the line. 'We can't let Spike get away!'

Stuart was quick to respond, leaping into action as soon as he realised what Spike had in mind. He joined Sparky on the line and the two boys ran along the sleepers as fast as they could, occasionally having to jump a gap where one was broken or missing.

Spike realised that he had been seen and he scrambled across the opposite platform before jumping down again onto the wide stretch of tracks where the carriages and waggons were stored.

Stuart and Sparky didn't once lose sight of him, even when he ducked below the level of the platform in a desperate attempt to shake them off his trail.

Spike reached the first line of railway waggons and disappeared briefly behind one of the trucks, pausing for a moment to decide the best method of escape. When Spike stopped, Stuart and Sparky stopped, tracking his every move, leaving nothing to chance. Then he was on the move again, and as Spike ran along one side of the trucks his pursuers kept pace on the other side. Suddenly, Spike changed direction and darted across the lines towards the great, black diesel engine which was standing in isolation near a steep section of banking.

Stuart knew exactly what Spike was going to do and as they ran towards him he shouted to Sparky: 'He's heading for the engine—if he climbs on top he can jump across to the banking and get away across the waste-ground! We're never going to catch him in time!'

The two boys stopped their chase and watched helplessly as Spike leapt onto the platform of the old engine. He hauled himself up to the top of the engine and stood upright ready to make the short leap across to the grassy bank.

'He's going to fall,' said Sparky, and he began to move slowly forwards towards the engine.

'What did you say?' asked Stuart. 'Did I hear you say . . . .'

'He's going to fall. That is quite correct—that is what I said.'

At that moment Spike turned to face his enemies, unable to resist a final taunt before completing his escape. He raised his hand to his mouth and blew a kiss to the helpless onlookers, but as he turned to make his jump his foot slipped on the greasy engine and he clutched frantically at the air in an attempt to save himself. It was no good. His legs buckled under him and he careered backwards, twisting in mid air to land with an almighty thud face down in the spreading pool of black, slimy oil.

Stuart and Sparky took one look at each other and burst out laughing. They laughed so much that their sides ached, and when they saw Spike doing his best to stand up in the slippery mess, falling over time and time again as his feet failed to grip, the oil covering him from

123

head to foot, the tears just rolled down their cheeks.

After several attempts to get to his feet Spike stopped struggling and sat down in the pool. He wiped the oil from around his eyes and looking over to Stuart and Sparky he asked pitifully: 'Aren't you going to help me, then?'

'Oh, I think you'd be better off staying where you are for a few minutes,' said Sparky, a broad grin on his face. 'You just sit and get your breath back while we go up on the footbridge to see how your friend Moggy is getting on.' And he turned and walked away, Stuart following behind as usual.

The footbridge was a rather ricketty structure that crossed the two main lines, joining the platforms and providing an excellent view far down the tracks. As the boys climbed the steps they could see that Moggy was still at large and P.C. Short was trying desperately to catch up with him as he dodged between the stationary railway waggons looking for a chance to make off down the line. Stuart and Sparky stood in the middle of the footbridge and followed the chase intently. It was like watching a game of cat and mouse. Moggy had positioned himself behind an open waggon and he was waiting for the policeman to make the next move. As soon as P.C. Short dashed to the side of the waggon Moggy was off again and across to the main line out of Thornley. It was obvious that he thought he could outrun P.C. Short and now that he was on the open line it seemed that nothing could stop him.

124

'He's going to get away,' said Stuart from the vantage point of the footbridge.

It was now quite dusk and the further Moggy moved away from the station the more difficult it became to make out his form.

'He won't get away,' said Sparky confidently. 'Look at the far end of the railway bridge.'

Stuart strained his eyes to see what it was Sparky had spotted.

'I can't see a thing,' he complained. 'How can you see anything with your eyesight? You can't see more than a couple of metres in front of you usually.'

'Keep watching,' said Sparky. 'You'll see what I mean.'

Moggy was still running down the line towards the bridge with P.C. Short giving chase, losing ground all the time. He was halfway across the bridge when he suddenly dug his heels in and ground to a halt, for walking steadily towards him from the other side of the bridge were two policemen, and closing in from behind was P.C. George Short, determined not to let the youth slip past him.

Moggy was trapped. He looked wildly to his right and then to his left. He was boxed in—there was no way of escape. But like a cornered animal he resolved to continue the fight and he grabbed from the track a stout piece of wood which he swung above his head like a club. The policemen kept walking, more slowly now, but never faltering in their approach.

'Keep away!' yelled Moggy. 'You keep away—do you hear?'

The police were on the bridge and still walking.

'Don't come any closer!' he screamed, brandishing the club above his head. 'You keep away from me!'

Still the police moved forward, and seeing that his warnings were being ignored Moggy panicked and leapt up onto the narrow bridge wall. P.C. Short raised an arm as a signal for his colleagues to stop, and taking a cautious step forward he said: 'Don't be stupid, lad—you've got to come down sooner or later.'

'You're not taking me!' screamed Moggy. 'You keep away!'

'Come on, lad—it's no use—give yourself up quietly.'

'I'm warning you—keep clear!' screamed Moggy, and he swung the club viciously, so viciously that he lost his footing and swayed dangerously on the crumbling wall. He fought with himself desperately trying to regain his balance, but it was no good and he reeled backwards with a piercing scream that travelled right along the line to where Stuart and Sparky watched in horror from their position on the footbridge.

P.C. Short rushed forward and peered over the bridge wall to the banking far below. He turned to face his colleagues with a grim look on his face and said: 'You'd better send for an ambulance. I'll go and sort out the other two.'

Fifteen minutes later Stuart, Sparky and P.C. Short were

standing in the station waiting room faced by boxes and boxes of stolen property.

'Well, I don't know where you two got all your information from,' said the bewildered policeman, 'but I suppose I'd better say thank you. We weren't getting very far with this case until you came along—in fact, we were getting quite . . . .'

'Embarrassed about it,' completed Sparky. 'Yes, I realise that, but I really think we'd better go home now and leave you and your colleagues to tidy up here. Stuart's parents will be getting worried—I'm sure you understand.'

And Sparky walked out of the waiting room with Stuart following behind as usual.

11

The Boy in the Photograph

'What did your parents have to say?' asked Michael as he and Stuart waited in the school yard for the morning bell to sound. 'Didn't they go mad at you for getting into trouble?'

Stuart looked pale and tired but he did his best to appear cheerful.

'They were a bit annoyed at first,' he admitted, 'but they soon came round. Anyway, I didn't really get into trouble, did I? The police said we were a great help, you know.'

Stuart was not telling the whole truth. His parents had been worried sick when he hadn't arrived home by dusk the previous evening, and when they received a phone call from the police explaining what was happening, they were still not reassured that their son was safe. They had gone straight down to Thornley Police Station where P.C. Brock was able to put their minds at rest. Stuart and Sparky had arrived back at the station about nine thirty, but it was nearly midnight by the time the police had finished asking questions and taking statements.

During all this time efforts to contact Sparky's father had failed, and when Stuart eventually left the station, pale and exhausted, Sparky was still chatting away to P.C. Short, full of life despite the exacting events of the day.

'Where's the other hero, then?' shouted Jenny, coming across the playground to join them. 'Is he too shy to show his face, or something?'

'I don't know,' replied Stuart, taking it for granted that Jenny was referring to Sparky. 'He didn't call for me this morning. Maybe he's not so well.'

'Anyway, this place should be a little more peaceful now that Spike's not around,' said Michael. 'I can't see many people missing him.'

'You've got to hand it to Sparky,' said Jenny, 'his "feelings" turned out to be right, didn't they?'

'I suppose so,' admitted Michael reluctantly. 'But I still think he's a nutcase. Anyway, it doesn't say much for the police if they couldn't work out that somebody called Moggy was a cat burglar!'

'It will be interesting to hear what Wacky has to say this morning,' said Jenny. 'Spike wasn't exactly his favourite pupil.'

As it happened, Wacky Watson had very little to say. After registration he commented that the police had detained some suspects in connection with the school break-in, but he did not mention Spike's involvement or the fact that Stuart and Sparky had been responsible for the suspects being apprehended.

Sparky still hadn't arrived at school by the time registration was completed and Stuart assumed that the strenuous events of the previous day had all been too much for him. It was only after assembly when the first lesson was well under way that Stuart realised something was wrong. Wacky Watson had settled the class down to some maths and Stuart was just struggling with a page of problems when Wacky approached him.

'Stuart—leave that for a moment, will you, and clear out Simon Parks' desk. Take all the books out to the front together with any of his personal belongings.'

Stuart put his pencil down immediately, a shocked expression on his usually cheerful face.

'What's wrong, sir?' he said in surprise. 'Why are you moving Sparky's things?'

'I'm sorry, Stuart,' said Wacky Watson sounding just as surprised. 'I assumed you knew—Simon won't be coming to St. Gregory's any more. His father has been moved again, urgently this time I believe. I should imagine Simon has already left Thornley by now. I'm just amazed the lad was so bright with having to move schools so many times.'

Stuart couldn't say anything for a moment; he sat there with his mouth open, a look of utter amazement on his face. He had realised that Sparky's stay in Thornley probably would not be permanent—Sparky had told him that much himself—but he hadn't expected his departure to be so sudden.

'Where's he gone to, sir?' asked Stuart, eventually finding his voice.

'I've no idea, I'm afraid,' replied Wacky. 'I don't know exactly what work his father does but it must be very important—secret, I mean—he's not even allowed to leave us a forwarding address.'

'I see,' said Stuart, and he looked at the empty seat beside him that had been occupied by the strange, red boy who kept playing with his glasses and finishing people's sentences for them. Maybe Michael was right—maybe he was a nutcase, but Stuart was going to miss him in spite of his peculiar ways.

For the rest of that morning Stuart found it very difficult to settle down to work. He kept thinking about the first day Sparky arrived, about the chewing gum stuck to P.C. Short's trousers, the rats that so nearly frightened him to death and the terrible moment when they saw Moggy fall from the railway bridge.

He felt no better at dinner-time. Stuart and Sparky had always sat together for their school dinner since Mr Boyling had moved Spike to a different place. Now there was a space next to Stuart, and to make matters worse it was spam fritters for dinner again. Stuart looked at his plate and couldn't help but picture Sparky's spam frisbee with a blob of pink bubble gum stuck to the middle of it. That incident had really marked the start of the feud with Spike, for although Sparky hadn't complained at the time it was something he didn't forget.

After dinner in the playground Stuart didn't know what to do with himself. Sparky had seemed to make things happen; he had brought a bit of interest and excitement to Thornley and now that he had gone things seemed pretty boring again.

Stuart cheered up a bit in the afternoon when Wacky

announced that they were going to work on their history project, but even this reminded him of Sparky and his uncanny knowledge of facts and details from the past.

The class split into groups as usual and Stuart, Michael and Jenny took out the large folder that contained pictures and news items about the war years taken from the *Thornley Chronicle*.

'Now where were we up to?' said Jenny looking at her notes.

'We'd just finished reading about the night the ammunition train was bombed,' said Michael. 'Sparky went off into one of his weird trances if you remember—started muttering about how horrible it all was.'

'I wouldn't mind having another look at those articles,' said Stuart. 'Especially after seeing the station and the railway bridge where it all happened.'

'Let's have a look then,' said Jenny, and she sorted through the pile of cuttings until she came to the edition of the *Thornley Chronicle* dated 5th September, 1940. There was the heading in bold, black type:

'AMMUNITION TRAIN HIT—HUGE EXPLOSION.'

Stuart read the article with renewed interest and he studied the picture which showed the remains of the train balanced precariously on the ruined bridge.

'It's incredible,' he said. 'The part of the bridge nearest to the station was blown away completely. It

132

must have taken them ages to rebuild.'

'It's a good job they did rebuild it,' said Michael, 'otherwise Moggy wouldn't have been able to fall off it.'

'Anyway, let's move on a bit, shall we?' said Jenny, and she turned over the paper even though Stuart hadn't really finished looking at it.

The same issue of the *Thornley Chronicle* contained a series of articles and photographs about the way the war affected local children. One photograph showed a group of children practising their air raid drill. The children were marching in straight lines down to the local churchyard where rows of Anderson shelters had been erected. They were carrying small boxes which Stuart remembered contained their gas-masks—Sparky had explained that to him. The clothes they wore looked very old-fashioned. Jenny laughed at the boys who all wore short trousers and had funny caps on their heads.

'I know Sparky said it would have been horrible,' commented Jenny, 'but I can't help feeling it must have been exciting.'

Another picture showed a group of boys playing football on the Parish Mill Fields.

'I'm sure that's the same pitch we played on last week,' said Stuart. 'Look at the shorts on them—they're down past their knees!'

'They look ridiculous,' said Michael. 'I don't know how they could run wearing shorts like that!'

Jenny was just about to turn the page when Stuart grabbed her arm. There was something about the picture that had caught his attention.

'Let me see that again,' he said, and he pulled the newspaper towards him so that he could take a closer look. Stuart stared down at the page in front of him. He looked up at Jenny and Michael, a strange expression on his face and then he stared down at the paper again.

'What's the matter?' asked Michael. 'You look as though you've seen a ghost. Your face has gone a funny colour. Are you feeling all right?'

'I think so,' said Stuart, 'but take a look at this.' He passed the paper back across the table so that Michael and Jenny could see more clearly, and leaning over he pointed to a boy who was standing all alone at the side of the pitch watching the game.

Jenny and Michael stared hard at the paper. The picture was quite clear despite its age, and as the boy had been facing the camera he could be seen in some detail. He was very thin, so thin that his clothes didn't seem to fit him properly. His jacket appeared to be far too big and the sleeves hung loosely over his hands. He was wearing a pair of round spectacles that seemed to be only just balanced on the end of his nose, and he was standing with both hands planted firmly in the pockets of his short trousers.

'It can't be,' said Michael quietly. 'If I didn't know better I'd say that was . . . .'

'Sparky!' completed Stuart. 'It looks exactly like Sparky—even the glasses look the same!'

'But we know it can't be Sparky,' said Jenny, still

134

staring at the photograph. 'That picture was taken nearly fifty years ago.'

'No, of course it can't be Sparky,' said Stuart, a thin smile appearing on his face. 'Sparky didn't know Thornley—he'd never been here before, remember?'